Floral Treasures of Japan

The Satsuki Azaleas

Floral Treasures of Japan

The Satsuki Azaleas

Alexander Kennedy

Splatt Press

First published in Great Britain in 1997 by
Alexander Kennedy,
Splatt Pottery, Tresmeer,
Launceston, Cornwall PL15 8QX

First published in the United States in 1997 by
Stone Lantern Publishing Co
P.O. Box 816
Sudbury, MA 01776

Copyright © 1997 Alexander Kennedy

All rights reserved. No part of this publication may be reproduced, stored in a retrieval system or transmitted in any form or by any means, electronic, mechanical, photocopying, recording or otherwise without the prior written permission of the copyright owner.

ISBN 0 9525145 2 4

Printed in Hong Kong by
Regent Publishing Services Ltd

Contents

What are Satsuki?	9
Wild Origins and Relatives	21
Satsuki in the Garden	33
Satsuki as Bonsai	43
Satsuki Flowers	53
Kanuma - Home of Satsuki	75
Satsuki Festivals and Exhibitions	85
Satsuki Growth and Pruning	97
Satsuki Propagation	123
Creating a Satsuki Bonsai	133
Cultural Requirements	155
Popular Satsuki Varieties	167
Further Reading	192
Glossary	192
Index	194

Introduction

When I wrote my first book, "Satsuki", in 1995, I did so to fill what appeared to me to be an urgent need. This need was for a fairly comprehensive English-language guide to the technical aspects of caring for these plants. While a number of valuable magazine articles were available , there was no single source, at that time, where English-speaking enthusiasts could look for information on Satsuki culture.

Awareness of, and interest in, Satsuki have grown rapidly since that first book was published. This new volume is intended to fulfil a rather different need, which is to provide a more wide ranging background to Satsuki. I hope that this book will appeal to the more general reader, as well as to the committed enthusiast.

The description of Satsuki as "Floral Treasures of Japan" has long been used by western horticulturists. In his Introduction to the 1984 English translation of "A Brocade Pillow" (the classic book on Japanese azaleas by Ito Ihei), the eminent American plantsman John L. Creech described Satsuki as Japan's most precious garden offering to the West. In 1997, awareness of this precious offering is still limited but is surely destined to grow in the coming years.

This book is broadly divided into three sections. Chapters 1 to 7 present a description of Satsuki and their history, together with an indication of their place in Japan today. Chapters 8 to 11 cover some of the many practical aspects of caring for these wonderful plants, while the final chapter 12, presents photographs and descriptions of some of the Satsuki most readily available in the west.

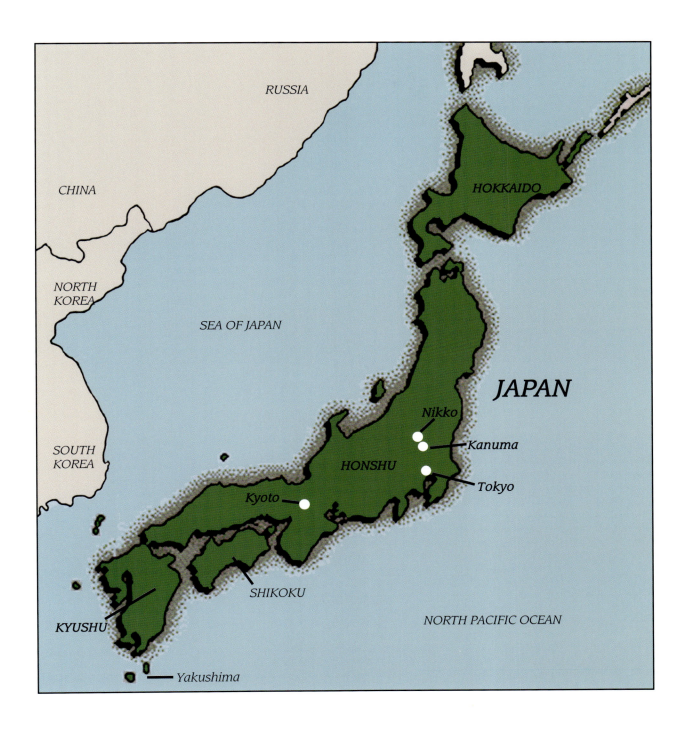

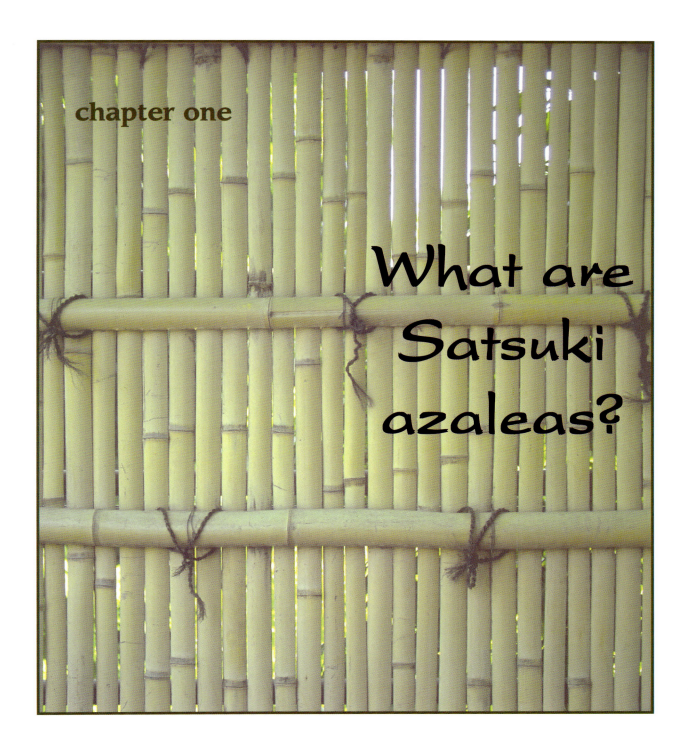

chapter one

What are Satsuki azaleas?

The Pot-grown Flowering Plant Raised to its Highest Level

The Satsuki azalea holds a very special place in Japanese horticulture. The growing of these azaleas, which have been bred and selected for over 300 years as container grown show plants, has long been a feature of Japanese culture. It is a hobby that attracts all classes in Japanese society including major figures in business and politics.

While most Japanese people grow Satsuki purely for their own pleasure, displaying these plants in public exhibitions or festivals is also very common. In Japan, there are growers for whom the gaining of prizes in shows is a central ambition in life. Many western gardeners who exhibit at flower shows could readily identify with these Japanese counterparts. Many Japanese spend countless hours tending chrysanthemums, lilies and other plants, while preparing them for show.

At the pinnacle of competitive plant culture in Japan stands the Satsuki azalea. Satsuki can be developed as large, stunning show plants which can stand comparison with all other container-grown plants for the variety of form and colour of

OPPOSITE: *A large plant of the variety* **Kogetsu-no-Homare** *in full flower.*

RIGHT: *A Satsuki bonsai of the variety* **Kaho**.

their beautiful blooms. Satsuki plants have additional interest in that they are very long-lived, woody, perennials which can continue in cultivation for centuries. They are capable of being improved and developed over many years and decades, and renowned old plants are styled as bonsai which can be fabulously valuable. Satsuki culture often inspires a fierce passion in those who adopt it as a hobby.

Satsuki Bonsai of the variety **Komei**.

Japanese people tend to take their hobbies very seriously indeed and any leisure activity is also likely to be a big business. The Japanese Satsuki hobby is able to support a considerable publishing industry, including a 150-page, monthly, full-colour magazine devoted to just this one plant.

One reason why Satsuki culture attracts fanatical hobbyists, alongside the more normal types, is that it offers so many complexities in which the true enthusiast can immerse himself (most, though by no means all, committed Japanese growers, are currently men). When such enthusiasts meet, there are many possible aspects of their hobby which can form the basis of long conversations and arguments. Discussion of the many varieties, for instance, is an almost endless subject for Satsuki growers. Current Japanese variety dictionaries describe and illustrate nearly one thousand different varieties in current cultivation.

All hobbies have their own secret store of lore and esoteric language which helps the true enthusiast to identify one of his own kind. Japanese growers use special names to describe over 20 different Satsuki flower markings. Such complexity is, of course, difficult for the beginner, especially if he or she does not speak Japanese, but such subtleties are undeniably a reason why many enthusiasts become hooked. In extreme cases, the Satsuki enthusiast can seem almost the horticultural equivalent of the anorak-wearing trainspotter; but thankfully, most growers are able to appreciate the intricacies of this fascinating hobby without quite losing their sense of proportion.

The Introduction of Satsuki to the West

Anyone who has seen a display of quality Satsuki azaleas in full flower will testify to their great beauty. Many visitors to Japan in early June have been stunned by the impact of a Satsuki exhibition seen there. These pampered aristocrats of the Japanese azalea world can rival any other container-grown show plant for sheer floral impact, while offering the connoisseur and enthusiast endless subtle variety

The massive and beautiful trunks developed by large Satsuki set them apart from other container-grown azaleas.

in form and colour variations.

Despite this, the very name Satsuki is still virtually unknown in the West outside the small circle of bonsai enthusiasts. Satsuki have had a number of champions over the years, particularly in the USA, but they have all too often been seen as merely one more group of garden azaleas. John L. Creech, a former director of the U.S. National Arboretum and past president of the American Horticultural Society played a great part in introducing and popularising Satsuki in North America; but his description of Satsuki as Japan's most precious garden offering to the West disguised a crucial point: the fact that in Japan the exotic Satsuki hybrid is not primarily a garden flower at all; it is a pot-plant.

Azaleas are of course commonly grown as pot-plants in the West. The "Belgian" forcing azaleas sold around Christmas are very distant relatives of the Japanese Satsuki. Attractive though these small commercial plants may be, however, it is severely stretching terminology to consider a fine large exhibition Satsuki as a mere "pot-plant" in the same sense.

A view of the gardens in the Renge-ji Temple, Kyoto, showing garden Satsuki plants clipped into rounded mounds.

Colour in the Traditional Japanese House and Garden

The very austerity of the traditional Japanese home and garden has given the seasonal pot-plant an important role. Japanese gardens take many forms, but colour is an aspect that is always carefully controlled, and usually very restrained.

A key theme in the design of both homes and gardens, indeed of all Japanese culture, is bringing out the distinction between the transient and the permanent. The basic structure of a typical Japanese garden is unchanging and understated, with colour schemes based on the deep greens of evergreen shrubs and the greys of rocks. Set against this, stronger colour is used for the transient elements which indicate the passage of the seasons. When flowering plants are used within a garden scheme, they are generally limited in area, variety

The Japanese Garden is typically austere with regard to colour. The emphasis on form and texture gives these gardens a timeless quality.
(Renge-ji Temple, Kyoto)

16

Many Japanese do not have gardens. When not in flower, plants are stored on roofs, or in small backyards, which are often packed to overflowing.

and number, so that they stand out in contrast to the overall scheme. This is a view of colour where the multicoloured flower-bed is an alien thing.

This alternative use of flowers was brought home to me the first time I visited a friends home near Osaka many years ago. The traditional Japanese house had an old traditional garden with no plants in flower, only green clipped-shrubs and grey rocks, surrounded by the browns of weathered wood and the paler shades of bamboo. In all this garden the only bright colour was a tiny pink primula growing in a pot, which had been placed next to the stone water basin. The impact of that small, carefully placed plant was astonishing. In some ways, it said more about the power of colour than all the bedding plants in a British public park could ever do.

The Japanese do love the brilliant colours of nature. Yet gorgeous displays of colour seem to be particularly enjoyed when they last only a few days. The annual sequence of Ume (plum blossom), Sakura (cherry Blossom), and Tsutsuji (azalea), through to the autumn brilliance of the Momiji (Japanese maple) is still very important to

The Tokonoma or display alcove is the focal point of a traditional Japanese room. The hanging scroll and other display items are changed regularly to indicate the passing seasons.

most Japanese people. These are not only, or even primarily, seen as displays of pretty flowers. They are important reminders of mortality and passing time.

Like the garden, the Japanese living-room is traditionally a very austere place, with colour restricted to the natural materials used in its construction. The focal point of such a room is the Tokonoma, or display alcove. Within this alcove would be displayed a hanging scroll, together with one or two other items. Possible display items could range from antique ceramics to viewing stones and from Bonsai to Ikebana, or pot-plants. A crucial point about the Tokonoma display is that it is a very temporary arrangement. Once again, the aim is to symbolise the passage of time and the seasons. Every month or so, the scroll and accessory items are changed for new ones appropriate to the time of year. And around early June, a Satsuki in flower has long been a favourite choice for display in the Japanese home.

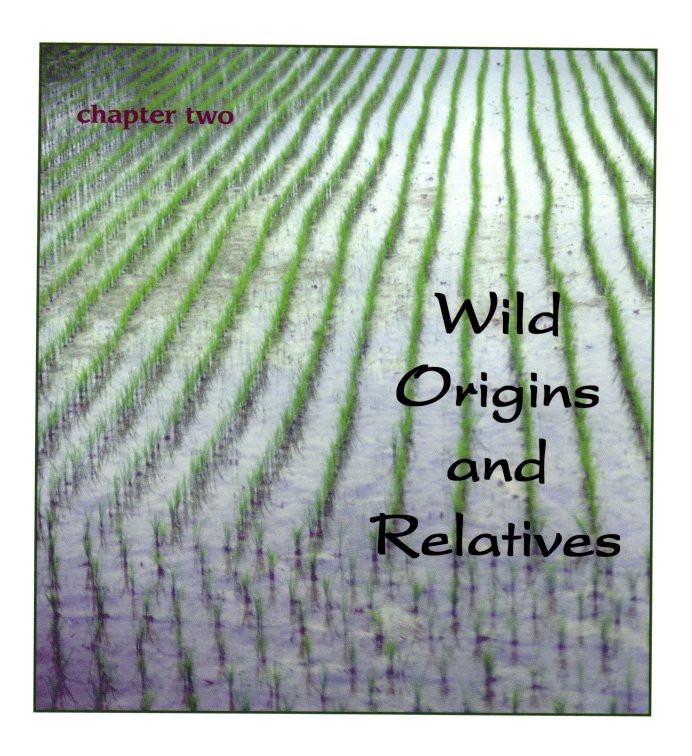

chapter two

Wild Origins and Relatives

Beginnings

The 1600's were a time of peace in Japan. With the whole country united under the rule of the Tokugawa Shogunate, it was the first extended period in over three hundred years where the land saw no civil war. Cities grew rapidly, and within these cities the merchant classes began to accumulate great wealth. They soon began to look for new ways to spend their riches. Powerful Samurai, deprived of the wars which had provided their purpose in life, sought hobbies to fill their new leisure-time.

Interest in gardening and the growing of plants exploded. A massive garden supply industry was born, the first anywhere in the world. Collectors were sent far and wide to find plants for sale, especially rare or unusual varieties.

While Japanese gardens were generally austere and concerned with form, a great love of flowers and colour was expressed through the cultivation of container plants. The chrysanthemum and the azalea became the favourite subjects for pot-culture. Many feudal lords became avid collectors of pot plants, but this was something that ordinary townspeople could also do, even those with no garden. A great pot-plant boom ensued.

The Great Azalea Vogue

By the late seventeenth century, dealers throughout Japan were selling many hundreds of different varieties and types of azalea. Many of these were garden plants, but others were already recognised as being ideal for pot-cultivation.

What came to be known in Japan as the great *Azalea Vogue* is first documented in the 1660's. A book on azaleas entitled ***Kadam Komoku*** was written in 1661 (though it was not printed until 1681). The book lists 147 varieties of azalea of which a few are believed to be Satsuki.

Ito Ihei

As interest in azaleas snowballed, there was a great rush to introduce new varieties to the marketplace. With so many new varieties being sold, confusion reigned over correct identification and naming. And so a Tokyo nurseryman named Ito Ihei decided to write a book which would help growers to identify their azaleas. Ito was widely known as an authority on azaleas and was commonly referred to by his nickname "Kirishima-san" or Mr. Kirishima (Kirishima was the name of one of the popular azaleas at that time). In 1692, Ito published the first volume of Kinshi Makura ("A Brocade Pillow") the world's first major horticultural book dedicated to a single group of plants. The book's five volumes, with profuse woodblock illustrations, described some 337 azaleas, of which 162 were Satsuki.

The type of illustration used by Ito Ihei in his historic book on azaleas.

Ito's book made the crucial division of Japanese azaleas into two groups: the Tsutsuji and the Satsuki. The Tsutsuji included all the spring-flowering azaleas and were basically garden plants. The Satsuki hybrids, however, which flowered around early June, were commonly grown in containers and could be placed on special display when they were at their flowering peak.

Ito was not the first to use the term Satsuki in print. It is first found in a book on flower arranging from 1684, but Ito is credited as the person who documented, if not invented, the clear distinction between Satsuki and other Japanese azaleas. It should be noted that it is the word Tsutsuji that Japanese speakers translate into English as "azalea". By setting Satsuki apart from all the others they were marked out as something special.

The word Satsuki consists of two Japanese Kanji characters; "Sa", which is an old term for five, and "Tsuki", which is the word for moon. Satsuki therefore means fifth moon, in other words the fifth month of the oriental lunar calendar. This is equivalent to around June in the western calendar, and refers to the flowering period. The majority of Satsuki flower between mid-May and mid-June. The meaning of the term Satsuki is rather deeper than this simple description of the flowering date, however. Some Satsuki have flowering periods which overlap with those of azaleas classed as Tsutsuji, yet the distinction is maintained. From the first Satsuki were very special show plants.

Large flower shows were already established in Japan by the early eighteenth century, and the beginning of June became a time of year associated with great Satsuki festivals. Such exhibitions were the forerunners of the great Satsuki shows of today.

The variety of different flowers seen in today's Show Satsuki have been developed over centuries of careful selection and breeding.

Wild Origins

Satsuki hybrids are primarily derived from two wild plants. These are Rhododendron indicum (also known as R. lateritum), and Rhododendron tamurae (also known as R. eriocarpum).

Rhododendron indicum

R. indicum is commonly known as **Kawa satsuki** (river satsuki) in Japan. References to this plant can be found in literature as early as the year 759, though at that time it was referred to as *Iwa tsutsuji* (the rock azalea). This species is widely distributed throughout western and southern Honshu, together with the islands of Kyushu and Shikoku, and many of the smaller southern islands. The plant is most commonly found on the steep rocky areas of mountain river valleys. R. indicum tends to a sprawling, ground-hugging type of growth, but can reach up to four feet or so in height. The leaves are relatively long and narrow, and they are pointed. The flowers normally have five petals

The majority of Japan is mountainous. Apart from the highest peaks, the mountains are typically covered with dense vegetation. Rhododendron indicum is normally found along rocky riverbeds, where more rampant species cannot gain a foothold.

Wild indicum azaleas grow in tiny pockets of soil among rocks.

*This Satsuki cultivar (**Hinotsukasa**) has many similarities to the wild Rhododendron indicum.*

and five stamens and are of a reddish-pink or orange-pink colour. A blotch of deeper red is prominent on the top petal. It is said that many variations in flower type were once found in the wild, including occasional white-flowered plants. Centuries of plant collection by both professional plant hunters and amateur gardeners appears to have largely eliminated atypical plants, however. Selections of the species Rhododendron indicum are available to gardeners in the West, often under the name Macrantha.

There has been some confusion in the west regarding the natural habitat of Rhododendron indicum. Western horticultural textbooks refer to it as being a mountain plant and this has tended to give the impression that it might be a plant of alpine meadows. Terming it a mountain plant has also been difficult to reconcile with the common Japanese name which translates as "river Satsuki".

In fact R. indicum thrives only in a very specific niche. Fast flowing mountain rivers in Japan tend to cut deep gorges through the bedrock. The main slopes above these rivers are typically covered by thick forest or dense undergrowth. R. indicum cannot compete in such an environment, but between these densely carpeted slopes and the water there is often a narrow strip of bare rock where soil has collected only in small hollows and crevices. Trees are unable to gain a foothold in this area, and the River Satsuki is often the dominant species in this soil-deficient, rocky area.

The fact that R. indicum grows in isolated patches surrounded by bare rock has the effect of making the plant stand out spectacularly when in flower, even when seen from a considerable distance away. This fact alone probably accounts for the great love Japanese people have for this wild flower. Visitors to Japan in early June, who make the train journey up the Hida river gorge to the tourist city of Takayama, are rewarded with many excellent views of R. indicum in bloom. The patches of orange-red stand out strongly against the dark foliage, even when seen from a train window high above the river.

Rhododendron tamurae

Rhododendron tamurae is known in Japan as ***Maruba satsuki*** (round-leaved satsuki). It is found growing over a much more southerly range than R. indicum, being found on many of the small islands to the south of Kyushu. The distribution in earlier times seems to have been much wider than this. Japanese authorities certainly refer to the collection of many ***Maruba satsuki*** hybrids from the hills of southern Kyushu during the nineteenth century. Although the geographical ranges of R. tamurae and R. indicum overlap, they are only found growing alongside one another on rare occasions, because R. tamurae usually grows at a lower altitude than R. indicum (R. tamurae has been found growing prostrate on the beaches of Yakushima island). Where the two species do grow in close proximity, it is likely that they

*The old variety **Seidai** is said to be a natural hybrid, collected in the mountains of Kyushu.*

hybridise easily.

R. tamurae is a very low ground-hugging shrub that is unlikely to exceed one and a half feet in height. The Japanese name gives a clear indication of the most distinctive feature of the foliage, for the leaves are much wider and more rounded in shape than those of R. indicum. Various writers have mentioned wild plants having a wide range of flower colours, including red, purplish-red, pale pink, white and variegated. I have never had the opportunity to see R. tamurae growing in the wild, but every photograph I have ever seen shows a plant with pale purplish-pink blooms. Rhododendron tamurae does not appear to be available for sale to western gardeners. Western authorities have often cited popular azalea varieties such as **Gunpo** (**Gumpo**) and **Gunrei** as being selections of R. tamurae, but Japanese sources always state that they are seedlings produced by crossing R. indicum with R. tamurae.

The geographical locations in which the two wild species are found give clear clues to their hardiness and required growing conditions. The mountainous areas of Honshu where R. indicum is found would have a fairly similar temperature range to Britain, though without the occasional very cold winter temperatures that this country suffers. Sea level on Yakushima Island, on the other hand, is frost free and almost subtropical. Plants with a great deal of R. tamurae blood might be expected to have some hardiness problems. The other big difference in climate from Britain concerns rainfall and humidity. Yakushima and the other southern islands have steamy, wet summers. Even Honshu has much more humid summer weather with high rainfall levels. Winters on Honshu by contrast are drier than North West Europe.

A number of western horticulturists and botanists have been

somewhat dubious about Japanese explanations of the parentage of Satsuki hybrids. Experiments involving the crossing of R. indicum with R. tamurae plants have been carried out, but these have given rise to plants lacking many of the characteristics found within the modern Satsuki group. One suggested explanation is that modern wild populations of these species are much depleted and lack much of the genetic variation they might once have had. After all, these plants have had to survive for many centuries in a densely populated land full of enthusiastic gardeners and plant collectors. Observers have noted that while modern wild azalea populations show little variation, plants with unusual forms and colours have been found growing in gardens in the same locality.

The other obvious possibility to account for the characteristics of the modern Satsuki hybrid is that other species may have been involved in its development. Japanese sources do indicate that many plants were collected from the wild during the **Meji Period** (1867-1912), and that many of these were natural hybrids between **Maruba satsuki** and various other azaleas. There are also records of some Belgian-Indian hybrids beings used to produce new crosses around 1930. The variety Mme. Moreux is cited as a grandparent of a number of popular Satsuki including **Shinnyo-no-Tsuki** and **Yamato-no-Hikari**.

This Satsuki was spotted growing wild on a banking near the city of Takayama. This is probably not a true wild indicum, however. Man has almost certainly played some part in establishing this plant in its current situation.

Since most of the characteristics found in modern Satsuki are already present in the descriptions found in Ito's book, it is possible that a much more complex parentage was involved in producing the varieties available in those days than is normally acknowledged in Japan. What is certainly clear from studying Ito's work is that azalea hybridizers in seventeenth-century Japan had as much knowledge and skill concerning their craft as any horticulturist in the world today.

*This double-flowered Satsuki **Gyokurei** is said to be a cross between the Satsuki variety **Kaho** and the Belgian-Indian azalea hybrid "Mme Moreux".*

Chapter three

Satsuki in the Garden

Satsuki in the Garden

This book has so far implied that Satsuki have been bred and selected almost exclusively for use as container-grown plants. While this is largely true, it is important to acknowledge the use of Satsuki as garden plants, particularly since introductions of these azaleas to the West have been seen almost exclusively in terms of garden use.

Satsuki used as abstract sculpture. This is the "Shisen-do" garden in Kyoto.

Magaki Satsuki

There is one specific type of Satsuki that is used in the (Japanese) garden and which is quite distinct from the show hybrids. This is the *Magaki* (hedge) Satsuki, also known as the **Mie Satsuki**, since many were produced in Mie Prefecture.

Hedge Satsuki are the plants used to produce the clipped mounds in traditional Japanese gardens. While western horticulturists discuss the use of Satsuki in gardens in terms of their flowers, the Japanese put these plants to a use in which flowering performance is secondary.

The clipped azaleas, which are such a feature of traditional Japanese garden design, commonly serve as symbolic mountains, rocks, full-size trees, or islands. A few rounded green masses within an expanse of white sand can thus be viewed as a cluster of islands in a great ocean. Or a jumble of clipped bushes on a small garden hummock can symbolise a great, tree-covered mountain slope. Magaki Satsuki are favoured for this purpose because of their dense, fine

Clipped Satsuki. Kiyomizu temple, Kyoto.

growth and superb response to pruning. Another feature of the typical hedge Satsuki, which is much appreciated by Japanese gardeners, is its tendency to develop a rich wine-red, or purple, foliage colour when exposed to winter chill. This is a feature of Rhododendron indicum and is restricted to plants which bear reddish flowers. Plants with white flowers retain green leaves in these circumstances.

The majority of hedge Satsuki used in Japan seem to have just one particular shade of strong pink flowers which look very similar to the variety **Osakazuki**. Occasionally, an odd plant with white flowers is put into the arrangement to provide a contrast, both at flowering time and during the winter period. Hedge Satsuki which sport both pink and white flowers exist, but are not very common in old traditional

Bonsai connection:-

These clipped Satsuki are growing along one of the lanes of the famous Omiya Bonsai Village, near Tokyo.

36

gardens. Very rarely, a single, large expanse of Satsuki hedge can be seen with a mixture of different red and pink flower shades. While eye-catching, such combinations can appear quite discordant and not just to my western eyes. Even Japanese viewers tend to comment that such displays "look wrong".

The hedging Satsuki have found a whole new lease of life in recent decades through their use for modern city landscaping. Throughout Japan, they are the shrubs chosen for planting around public buildings, hotels, traffic islands, etc..

A key feature of the Satsuki growth pattern is that the plant puts on a strong flush of spring growth before flowering, which means that

Hedging Satsuki are the most commonly used city landscaping plant in modern Japan.

the flower buds are then submerged beneath the foliage. This allows the bush to be clipped to a smooth topiary type finish while still leaving a large number of the flowers intact.

Mie Satsuki appear to be selections of Rhododendron indicum rather than complex hybrids. Flower type, foliage and the tendency to colour-up in winter are all characteristics of wild indicum plants.

Massed, clipped Satsuki at the entrance to a shrine in Kyoto.

Show Satsuki in the Garden

A number of eminent writers on azaleas have stated that Satsuki may be Japan's most precious floral gift to the West. It is strange to note that such comments have always referred to show Satsuki and their potential for garden use. The show Satsuki has indeed become a valued garden plant in many parts of the United States. It offers an extension of the azalea flowering season into the summer months and very spectacular colour.

Of course, show Satsuki are and always have been grown in Japanese gardens. The Japanese use of such Satsuki is not the typical English massed azalea planting, however. Instead of attempting to overwhelm the senses with a wide-screen riot of colour, a Japanese gardener is likely to plant a single show Satsuki in isolation. The idea

*This ancient bonsai of the variety **Osakazuki** has almost certainly spent many years growing in a garden.*

is to focus attention on just one plant as a spectacular coloured gem against a setting of green.

All of the old, heavy-trunked Satsuki bonsai which are shown in Japan today have spent a long period of their lives growing in the ground. Large trunk dimensions can be developed only if the plants are allowed unrestricted growth in open ground. Today, large-trunked bonsai are developed in commercial nursery beds, but a large proportion of the biggest and most dramatic old trees have come from private gardens.

Japanese Satsuki magazines often illustrate the initial styling of trunks grown in open ground. In some of these cases, the large trunks

A large show Satsuki growing in a Japanese garden. This plant is probably the ancient variety **Sangosai**.

are reported to be bonsai which were planted out in gardens during the Second World War. Water was strictly rationed in Japan during the war and this led to many Satsuki collectors planting their trees out in the ground because of the difficulty in watering their plants. When such plants can be found and dug up today, they offer enormous trunk diameters. There are probably no other azaleas which even approach Satsuki in their capacity to develop very large trunks in this way. For visitors to a Japanese Satsuki exhibition, the sight of huge bonsai with trunks over 30cms in diameter is every bit as dramatic as the oceans of multicoloured flowers that confront them. Unfortunately, such plants are still unknown in the West except through magazine reproductions.

*A clipped azalea bush with multi-coloured flowers, but it is not a Satsuki. This is a **Tsutsuji** azalea in early April. This plant has a very similar parentage to many spring-flowering azaleas grown in western gardens.*

chapter four

Satsuki Bonsai

The Bonsai Influence

Many westerners think of all container-grown Satsuki as being bonsai, but the great majority of plants grown in Japan are not seen by their owners in these terms. Most Satsuki are grown primarily to provide a display of flowers and are mainly intended for viewing during the short flowering period. Yet throughout this century the concept of styling Satsuki as bonsai has been steadily spreading and

A root-over-rock style Satsuki shown at a Japanese exhibition.

continues to do so.

There is no clear date when Satsuki were first styled in the image of trees. It was almost certainly a gradual development rather than a sudden conscious decision. The Japanese often pick the year 1912 as a dividing line. This is not a year with any specific bonsai connections, rather it marked the end of the Meji era in Japanese history. Satsuki which date from before 1912 are often referred to as "natural" trees with the implication that their styling was less planned.

Many traditional bonsai styles have been modified when applied to Satsuki. This tree shows obvious connections with the traditional Literati style, but the large, flat lower foliage pad has been developed with flowering very much in mind.

Suitability for Bonsai Training

Satsuki plants have many characteristics which make them highly suitable for bonsai training.

Foliage

Leaves vary in size from variety to variety but all can be described as small or very small. This allows Satsuki to be developed as small bonsai without problems of the foliage looking out of scale. The rapid production of dense growth enables the quick and easy styling of convincing foliage pads.

When not in flower, the dark foliage of Satsuki bonsai is an excellent foil for other species with more exuberant leaf form or colour. On the other hand, when Satsuki bonsai are shown en masse the foliage can look rather heavy. The Japanese get round this by holding many Satsuki bonsai shows in the autumn when the plants are showing their typical two-tone leaf colour. Although they are evergreen, Satsuki develop two sets of leaves each year and the summer leaves turn to attractive yellows or wine reds before falling. Unfortunately, the weather plays a big part in determining how attractive this autumn transformation will be. Given sunny days and crisp autumn nights, most of the summer leaves will change colour at one time and provide an attractive display. If the autumn is mild, however, the leaves tend to

This tree clearly shows the use of bonsai styling principles, but elements of the older Meika style can still be seen.

change colour in dribs and drabs and merely look untidy. Late autumn is not a traditional time for bonsai shows in the West and most growers have failed to appreciate the potential beauty of a well prepared Satsuki in fall colour.

Trunk

Even if Satsuki did not flower at all, they would be valued by bonsai growers for their superb trunks. Satsuki naturally form well buttressed bases with attractive surface roots. With time, trunks of massive diameter can be grown with tremendous character and taper. Old bonsai with trunks up to 30cm diameter can be seen at the major Japanese shows where they are greatly revered. When such trees are sold they command fabulous sums from Japanese collectors and it is

Group planting styles are currently very popular in Japanese Satsuki exhibitions. Most plantings tend to be clump, or root-connected styles, rather than true groups.

unlikely that western growers will ever see such specimens except in reproduction. Good quality Satsuki trunks, albeit of more modest proportions, are now finding their way on to the western market, however, and their popularity can only continue to grow.

Bark

The bark of Satsuki trunks is another attractive feature. When the natural dark brown bark is regularly brushed and washed the smooth inner bark is revealed which can vary in colour from a mottled bronze or mahogany red through to pale greys or tans.

The beautiful bark quality of Satsuki trunks is one of their many attractions.

Response to pruning

In training a bonsai, the artist must adapt his (or her) vision to the characteristics of the species being worked on. The Satsuki growth habit has a number of valuable features which assist the training process.

Another Satsuki trained in the Literati style with the very popular large hanging branch.

Satsuki of any age can produce new shoots from any part of the plant. With skill and patience new branches can be grown from exactly the places dictated by the bonsai design. Such new branches can then be developed rapidly thanks to the vigorous shoot growth and rapid re-budding after pruning.

Satsuki Bonsai Today

Today, an increasing proportion of Japanese growers are setting themselves the task of styling their Satsuki to the highest standards expected of bonsai. Others, however, still compromise form for the sake of flowering performance, or settle for a mere outline form of a tree. Even where tree-forms are more sophisticated, some stylists have still to learn to avoid over-manicured or topiary-like effects, errors which are all too easy to fall into given the small-leaved and dense-growing nature of Satsuki.

Historically, Satsuki and bonsai have developed quite separately in Japan, each having its own institutions with the associated political hierachies. This has probably played a big part in keeping the Satsuki bonsai hobby somewhat distinct from mainstream bonsai. Nevertheless, Satsuki are now an essential feature of Japan's top bonsai exhibitions, such as the great **Kokufu** show held in Tokyo each year. Even today's greatest bonsai artist, **Masahiko Kimura**, best known for his pines and junipers, feels the need to tackle Satsuki styling as part of his all-round mastery.

While many Japanese Satsuki fall short of the sophistication common in other bonsai subjects, the best Satsuki bonsai present unforgettable images and can clearly stand up to being viewed alongside the great pines, junipers and maples.

In the West, bonsai growers were much slower to appreciate the potential of Satsuki as a subject for the creation of high quality bonsai. This was partly due to a lack of examples, something which has changed dramatically in the last few years with the reproduction of many fine specimens in magazines. The other problem has been the misapprehension that the large flowers somehow rendered these plants less suitable.

The important position of bonsai styling within the Satsuki world is demonstrated by the number of Japanese Satsuki exhibitions which are now held outside of the flowering season. In these exhibitions the tree form alone can be appreciated, without the distraction of flowers. Satsuki bonsai can never give a convincing impression of being large trees when in flower. Instead, they offer the potential to create a superb bonsai, which changes, for a few weeks each year, into one of the world's most spectacular flowering plants.

*Root connected group of the variety **Nyohozan**.*

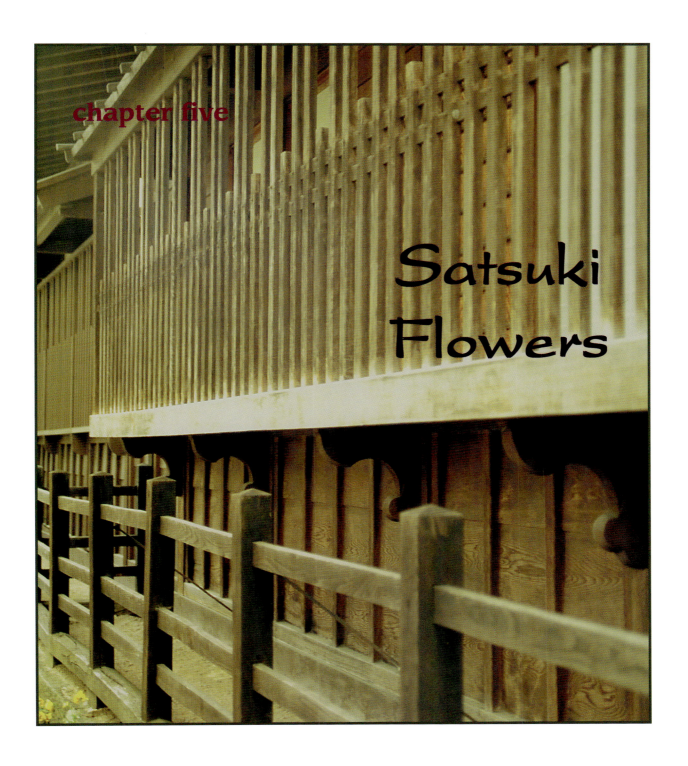

chapter five

Satsuki Flowers

The Satsuki Flower

The typical Satsuki flower has the same general structure as other azaleas. There are five petals which are fused together for some distance from the base and together form the corolla. The petals are arranged in what is often referred to as a "butterfly" structure. One petal (sometimes called the standard) points straight up. Beneath this the two upper wings extend outwards and usually form the widest part of the flower. The final two petals, or lower wings, extend downwards as well as out.

The female flower-parts spring from the centre of the corolla. These consist of the five-celled ovaries which have a hollow tube called the style extending out above them and terminating in the stigma, or pollen receptor. The male flower parts, or stamens, arise between the base of the ovaries and the corolla. Again there are typically five of these stamens and they are normally of differing lengths.

Beneath the corolla is the calyx, which consists of five small green sepals, largely fused together. The calyx is a rather small and fairly insignificant structure on the typical Satsuki flower.

Cross-section of a Satsuki Flower

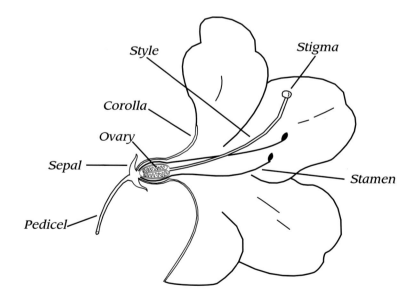

Attaching the calyx to the plant stem is the pedicel or flower-stem. Pedicel length varies considerably with the variety but can be 2-3 cms in many cases. This helps to raise the flowers clear of the dense Satsuki foliage, which has often put on considerable spring growth before the flowering period.

Flower Types

Few groups of flowering plants have such a long history of careful and skilled selection and breeding as Satsuki. It is not surprising that after some 350 years of such selection, Satsuki hybrids now offer a very wide range of flower size, form and colour.

While the typical Satsuki flower still has the five petals of the original wild parents, there is enormous variety in the possible petal forms. More extreme variations include both semi-double and double-flowered types, as well as hose-in-hose forms. A wide variety of flowers with unnaturally narrow petals are also found. At their most extreme, such flowers are referred to as **Saizaki**, (Sai or Zai means tassel), the most popular variety of this type being **Kinsai**.

Carrying such distortion even further than **Kinsai**, there are

The classic saizaki variety,
Kinsai.

Shiryu-no-Homare

varieties such as *Shiraito-no-Taki*, in which the petals are almost entirely absent on most flowers, only stamens and pistils being visible. It would be quite reasonable to expect that such an extremely distorted form could never be more than a botanical curiosity. In fact, a fine specimen of *Shiraito-no-Taki* in full flower is a very attractive plant. A delicate white mist of flowers covers the dark-green foliage and brings home the appropriateness of its Japanese name "White-Thread-Waterfall.".

At the other end of the spectrum are the very large full-petalled forms. Some varieties of this type, such as *Shuku-fuku*, *Tama-no-hada* and *Hi-gasa* have blooms up to 12cm or more in diameter and can have an almost circular tea-plate shape.

In addition to variation in their overall shape, Satsuki petals vary greatly in curvature, texture and smoothness or frilliness of outline.

The large blooms of the variety **Hi-gasa**. *The name means Parasol.*

*The subtle variety, **Bunka**, has long been a favourite with people who find multicoloured Satsuki excessive.*

Satsuki with double or semi-double flowers are regularly seen in Japan though they do not appear to be hugely popular. Varieties of this type are not easily found in the West, but the red-flowered **Yaegoromo** and **Beni-Botan** and the white **Hana-Botan** are among those available.

A double flower is formed when the stamens are fully transformed into petals. A semi-double is defined as one where this transformation is incomplete, the resulting petals being smaller than the true petals, or still having some stamen-like structures.

Another aberrant flower structure of note is the hose-in-hose type. This is produced when the sepals are transformed into another set of petals, giving the effect of one flower inside another. Only one Satsuki variety of this type is popular today, but it is a very beautiful plant and well suited to bonsai training. This is the pink-flowered **Wakaebisu** which will hopefully become more freely available in the West.

Contrasting flower forms. Left, **Chigosugata**; *Right,* **Korin**.

Flower Colour

The wild Rhododendron indicum generally has flowers of a pale orange-red or reddish-pink colour though occasional plants bear white blossoms. Rhododendron tamurae flowers are typically a purplish-pink colour, but blooms of red, white and varied pinks are all said to occur.

In modern Satsuki hybrids the colour range extends from orange, through pink and red, to crimson and purple, as well as white. There are no blues or true yellows to be found among the evergreen azaleas, though efforts are being made to produce more yellowish shades. Satsuki do not produce any really dark-coloured blooms but deeper, more saturated reds and purples are being bred. The American-bred

The attractive hose-in-hose variety, **Wakaebisu**.

hybrid named **Polo** features one of the most intense scarlet-red shades to be found in a Satsuki.

Despite the limitations, the colour range available in Satsuki is very rich. This colour variety is made even richer by the fact that combinations of colour on one plant and even on one flower are very common.

One of the Satsuki varieties with intense purple flowers which are currently popular in Japan.

Flower Patterns

The range of beautiful colour markings to be found on Satsuki blooms is vast. The study and identification of these many flower patterns is complex and can be a quite addictive hobby in itself. The Japanese distinguish and name over twenty different multi-colour patterns, in addition to solid-coloured flowers (selfs), which may themselves have a throat blotch in a darker or contrasting colour. To uneducated western eyes, some of these colour patterns can look remarkably similar, but learning to spot and distinguish the many subtle variations is one of the joys of these beautiful plants.

White self

Ground Colour

The ground colour, or underlying background colour, is typically white, red or purple. Flowers with only one solid colour (with or without a blotch) are referred to as selfs. In Japanese, the term **muji** is added to the colour to indicate a self; e.g. **Aka-muji** (red-self), **Shiro-muji** (white-self), **Murasaki-muji** (purple-self).

Red self

61

Pink Ground (Jiai-zaki)

Interestingly, the Japanese do not consider pink to be a base-colour in the same way. It is seen as a combination colour (*Jiai*) from two base colours, red and white. Pink-ground flowers are referred to as *Jiai-zaki*. The *Jiai-zaki* variety most commonly seen in the West is **Gyoten**, the pink-ground sport of **Kaho**.

Pink self

Blotch Colour

The blotch is a pattern of dots on the standard, or top, petal and often spreading out onto the two upper wings. The blotch can be lighter or darker than the ground. It can also be of a contrasting colour. On many multi-colour plants, the white flowers have a green blotch, while the pink-ground flowers have a crimson blotch.

Blotch

Colour-Ring Variations

This term refers to those flower types which have broadly circular patterns around the centre of the flower.

Sokojiro

Sokojiro or White-Throat

The flower has a white circular centre surrounded by a continuous border of a darker colour. Typical varieties with **sokojiro** flowers include **Seidai** and **Hiodoshi**.

Satsuki branches with any of the colour-ring variations tend to flower true to type. On a few varieties, however, an occasional flower will appear which has a basic **sokojiro** pattern but with a sector of the flower overlaid by a striped or flecked pattern. **Kagetsu** is one variety which shows this mixture, known as **Shibori sokojiro** (variegated sokojiro).

Tsumabeni

Tsumabeni (crimson fingernail)

This is a pattern where the white **sokojiro** centre of the flower has expanded to cover all but the tips of the petals.

Fukurin or Shirofukurin (White jewel border)

This pattern is commonly described as being the opposite of *sokojiro*. With *fukurin* the darker-coloured centre of the flower is surrounded by a white margin. While the dark border in *sokojiro* describes a circle around the centre of the flower, the white border in the *fukurin* pattern follows the shape of the petals. The inner edge of the white margin usually forms a serrated pattern with the ground colour. The white margin can be very narrow or quite wide and prominent. *Fukurin* is not the type-flower of any variety, but is a form that occurs in a great many of the multi-pattern varieties, e.g. *Kogetsu* and *Chiyo-no-Homare*.

In some varieties, a white margin occurs only at the tips of the petals. This pattern is known as *Tsumajiro* (white fingernail) and is the opposite of *Tsumabeni* described above.

Fukurin

Janome-shibori (bull's eye variegation)

On some varieties with mixed flower-patterns, blooms occur with a white *fukurin* border superimposed on a white-centred *sokojiro* flower. This gives an effect of bull's eye concentric circles.

Janome-shibori

Tamafu (white jewel spot)

While not strictly a colour-ring pattern, **Tamafu** is related to the above forms. In this pattern, each petal fades from deep margins to a pale, or white centre. The typical flower of this pattern is found on the variety *Yata-no-Kagami*.

Note: While the true sokojiro form is supposed to have a round white centre, there appears to be a continuous range of variants between this round-centred form and the tamafu-type petal spots. The sokojiro flowers on a variety such as **Kogetsu** are really halfway between tamafu and true sokojiro.

Tamafu

Markings on the ground colour or Shibori

Most patterns on Satsuki flowers can be seen as flecks, patches or stripes of a darker colour on a white ground. These patterns are all referred to by the general term **Shibori**. When the darker patterns are on a pink ground they are referred to as *Jiai-shibori*.

The word *shibori* can be broadly translated as "variegation" but the real meaning is tie-dyed. This refers to the similarity between many Satsuki markings and the patterns produced by the traditional Japanese tie-dye textile process.

The traditional names given to the many, often fairly similar patterns, brings out the great Japanese love of classifying things. Descriptions can be conveniently split into those covering large stripes of colour and those covering small speckles and flecks.

O-shibori
(See next page)

Stripes and Sectors

O-shibori (major sector variegation)

This is a pattern where at least half of the petal is coloured in the contrast colour. Often whole petals are coloured giving a very bold effect. The variety **Kogetsu** often features this type of flower. (See illustration on previous page.)

Hanzome

Hanzome (half-coloured)

When half or more of the flower is the darker contrast colour, it is referred to as *Hanzome* (half-coloured). The popular variety **Kaho** often features *Hanzome* blooms.

Ko-shibori (small, or minor sector variegation)

The petal is marked by small stripes of colour which are less than half the petal width. The stripes are roughly parallel to the centre line of the petal but do not extend all the way from edge to centre.

Ko-shibori

Tate-shibori

Tate-shibori (lengthwise variegation)

This is a similar pattern, but in this case the coloured sectors extend from the edge to the centre of the flower.

Daisho-shibori

Daisho-shibori

When both *O-shibori* and *Ko-shibori* occur on the same petal, the Japanese complicate matters further by naming the pattern *Daisho-shibori*.

Date-shibori (showy variegation)

Where the white ground of the entire flower is crowded with *Ko-shibori* type sectors, this is known as *Date-shibori*. The variety **Matsunami** bears many flowers of this type.

Date-shibori

Shiro-shibori (white variegation)

On a striped flower, deciding what is ground and what is contrast colour is often just a matter of convention. Where the darker colour covers most of the flower so that it resembles *Ko-shibori* patterns in reverse, the Japanese then refer to the pattern as *Shiro-shibori*.

Shiro-shibori

Speckles and Flecks

The range of different patterns produced on Satsuki flowers by fine stripes, flecks and dots is almost infinite. Below are just a few of the types which the Japanese have thought worthy of naming.

Hakeme-shibori

Hakeme-shibori

This is a pattern where the flower is covered in numerous, fine parallel lines. **Hakeme** is a type of coarse brush used to decorate pottery with a parallel-line pattern

Fukiage-shibori

Fukiage-shibori (fountain variegation)

A spray of fine streaks spreads out from the centre of the flower along each petal. The markings are densest in the centre of the petals and fade toward the edges.

Fukkake-shibori

Similar to *Fukiage-shibori* but the fine spray of specks and flecks are concentrated around the edges of the flower, fading into the centre.

Fukkake-shibori

Arare-shibori (hail variegation)

Many large-ish streaks and spots all over the petals.

Arare-shibori

Mijin-shibori

Mijin-shibori (fine-particle variegation)

A mist of innumerable fine particles all over the petals. The flower often looks solid pink from a distance.

Harusame

Harusame (spring rain)

A coarser version of the above, with specks and flecks covering the entire surface of the flower.

Different patterns may not only be found on different flowers on the same plant, they may even be found within one flower.

If the descriptions on the previous pages seem complex, it is also important to realise that these different patterns can not only occur together on the same plant, but can in some instances be combined on the same flower.

Some varieties seem to specialise in outlandish combinations. The variety ***Kanuma-no-Hikari*** is most notable in this respect, rarely producing two flowers with the same combination of patterns.

Maintaining colour patterns on a plant

A large majority of Satsuki growers in the West are dealing with relatively young plants. In many cases these growers are troubled by the fact that their bonsai bears mainly white flowers. A great fear for these people when it comes to pruning is that they might cut off the branches bearing the few coloured flowers their plant produces. They worry that if these branches were removed, the plant might never produce anything but white flowers again.

Losing coloured branches which are important to a design may be a great loss in the short term and this should be guarded against by marking the crucial branches at flowering time. In the longer term, however, these growers have little to fear. A typical Satsuki is almost guaranteed to produce more and more flowers bearing the contrast colour as years go by.

Where mature Satsuki are concerned, the problem becomes one of maintaining a suitable proportion of white flowers. This is something which greatly concerns Japanese growers though this is in part due to the fact that they seem to have very particular notions about what proportions of different coloured flowers look "correct".

The root of this long term problem is the fact that while branches bearing white or **_shibori_** flowers will gradually sport branches bearing red selfs and flowers such as **_sokojiro_** or **_fukurin_**; branches bearing the latter never revert to bearing flowers with a white ground. It is therefore inevitable that such plants will bear fewer and fewer white ground flowers as the years go by. Eventually, the grower has to take action to prevent the red ground flowers from taking over the whole plant. The cure is to selectively prune out branches bearing red, or colour-ring type flowers, and training white ground flowers to replace them.

chapter six

Kanuma – Home of Satsuki

A Town whose existence revolves around Satsuki

One Japanese name is inextricably linked with Satsuki. This is Kanuma, the place where Satsuki are grown and the source of the

Despite its relatively small size and rural position, the centre of Kanuma has an abundance of the grey concrete, jungles of overhead electric wires and huge advertising signs that can be seen throughout Japan. Yet, as everywhere in that country, pockets of great beauty can be discovered around almost any corner. The mountains of Nikko National Park can be seen in the distance.

Many drainage gutters on Kanuma city's streets are covered by cast iron gratings decorated with Satsuki flowers.
The design appears to be based on the illustrations in the ancient book by **Ito Ihei**.

special soil for Satsuki, which also bears the name Kanuma.

The city of Kanuma is small as Japanese cities go. While it now boasts electronic factories and many other manifestations of modern Japan, the impression remains distinctly rural. Kanuma is situated just outside the much larger city of Utsunomiya, just under one hour north of Tokyo by bullet-train and close to the mountains of Nikko National Park.

Although it is set in the shadow of a mountain range, the district itself is in a very flat alluvial plain. Much of the land is only a few feet above the level of the Kurogawa river, which flows through the centre of Kanuma. The name Kanuma means "Deer swamp city" and the many drainage ditches which cross the land can sometimes remind one of Holland.

Entrance to the Kanuma Satsuki Centre

Horticulture has long been the main industry in the area and a huge number of nurseries, both large and small, produce all types of ornamental shrubs, trees, flowers and vegetables.

The area is renowned throughout Japan for its Kanuma strawberries, but above all else, it is Japan's leading centre for the production of Satsuki azaleas.

The name Satsuki can be seen everywhere in Kanuma. Wandering around, one can see signs advertising "The Satsuki Bar" or "The Satsuki Restaurant". When I first visited Kanuma in 1994, there were posters everywhere advertising "The Satsuki Marathon", which is run through the city streets. Many official signs are

Just some of the vast stocks of bonsai containers on sale at the Kanuma Satsuki Centre.

decorated with Satsuki flowers and even the grilles covering the road drains have Satsuki designs on them(page77).

Satsuki nurseries lie all around the city. They range from small enterprises specialising in the production of Satsuki cuttings, to the giant nurseries which sell everything up to large exhibition specimens costing millions of Yen.

Visiting western bonsai enthusiasts once came to Kanuma in order to see a botanical park which featured a large collection of Satsuki. Unfortunately this park has now closed but its role has been largely taken over by another Satsuki Centre.

The Kanuma Satsuki Centre

The Kanuma Satsuki Centre is rather like a huge garden centre which is devoted primarily to Satsuki. It is a co-operative venture and many Satsuki nurseries in the area have plants on sale at this one site. Countless Satsuki can be seen on hundreds of display benches. Many other local horticultural products are also on display in addition to the Satsuki. These include alpines, locally-made stone lanterns and a whole gallery showing products from the local woodcarving producers.

When Japanese plant a garden they do not put in young saplings and wait for them to mature. Instead they buy full-sized trees and transplant these to the new site. At the Kanuma Centre there are stocks of these large trees which have been styled in a similar manner to bonsai and have had their roots regularly trimmed in preparation for moving.

The Satsuki Centre has large areas available for special exhibitions. Shows of bonsai, alpines, etc. take place throughout the year. At the end of May, the Centre is transformed when it hosts the Kanuma Satsuki Festival which is famous throughout Japan. For this event, most of the Centre's main car park is covered with display stands and traders stalls. The show lasts for 9 days and huge numbers

Part of the Satsuki sales area at the Centre.

of people attend from far and wide. Uniformed security guards direct traffic to the large temporary car parks and special shuttle-bus services bring visitors from the local train stations, or take them off to visit some of the big local nurseries.

The Satsuki Nurseries

The largest Satsuki nurseries in the Kanuma area would perhaps be better described as farms. Largest of all is the nursery called Takahashi Engei. The quantity of high-quality stock to be seen there is quite mind-numbing. Fields of Satsuki plants at various stages of growth stretch to the horizon and row upon row of polythene-covered

Tunnels packed with Satsuki at the Takahashi-Engei nurseries.

growing-tunnels spread in all directions. Satsuki which have been singled out for special attention are displayed in large, transparent-roofed sheds, or in small gallery areas. Very special guests are treated to tea in an upstairs room overlooking the nursery, where exquisite specimens are displayed, including unusual or rare varieties.

Of course, this is Japan, where the aim of a business is to make every visitor feel like a guest. As each car or coach drives into the parking area, Mr. Takahashi and all his staff stop what they are doing, bow to the newcomer and gave the obligatory "Irasshiamase" call of welcome.

While I saw large numbers of finished Satsuki bonsai on display at Takahashi Engei and at the other nurseries I visited, it was quite clear even from a short period of observation, that the majority of customers were looking for untrained trunks to style themselves.

Many of the untrained trunks available in Kanuma are of great size and superb quality. I was taken to see a field containing several

View over just part of the Takahashi-Engei nurseries.

*Right:-
Very large Satsuki trunks being grown-on in deep nursery beds at Takahashi-Engei.*

hundred large trunks. These belonged to Mr Kobayashi, another of the major nurserymen. He told me they were all around forty-five years old. Each one had been carefully maintained and pruned throughout its life to produce potential bonsai of the highest grade and many had trunks exceeding 20cms at the base. The trip to see that one field was enough to make my visit to Kanuma unforgettable.

chapter seven

Satsuki Festivals and Exhibitions

Exhibiting Satsuki

Whether they own a large and very famous old bonsai, or just a few thin-trunked flowering plants they have raised themselves, Japanese Satsuki enthusiasts love to show them off.

Satsuki shows appear in many different guises throughout Japan, from small neighbourhood events, to the large national shows which are covered by television and sponsored by Government. In some areas, annual festivals featuring Satsuki are a long-established tradition. This is particularly true in those parts of the country where raising Satsuki commercially has a long history.

Most of the smaller exhibitions which are held today, however, are staged by the many hundreds of local Satsuki societies which exist throughout the length and breadth of Japan. Small local shows of this type will often feature trees which would be the envy of growers in the West.

This huge billboard poster advertises Satsuki exhibitions throughout Japan during 1996. Each flower on the map represents a show.

At the opposite end of the scale are the big National shows. At flowering time there are major shows in many parts of Japan. Apart from the Kanuma Satsuki Festival, there is a famous exhibition held each year in the grounds of Nagoya castle. Above all others stands the National Satsuki Festival, which is staged by the Japan Satsuki Association in Tokyo at the beginning of June.

The Japan Satsuki Association also stages a National Satsuki Bonsai Exhibition, which is held in late October to early November in Kyoto. As the name suggests, the "Satsuki Bonsai Exhibition" is dedicated to those Satsuki which have attained a high level of Bonsai training. It is held at a time of the year when the trees have no flowers to disturb the contemplation of their treelike form.

*A trophy is the reward for the many hours of preparation put in by the owner of this **Meika** in the Tokyo National Festival.*

The "National Satsuki Festival" is the great jewel in the Japanese Satsuki calendar. For seven days the area around the Shinobazu Pond, in Ueno Park, Tokyo is transformed. Long runs of covered staging are erected to display the finest Satsuki from throughout Japan. The scale of this show is stunning considering that it is devoted to just one type of potted plant. As would be expected of a big event in Japan, everything is presented in a very slick fashion, with a team of very attractive young ladies in smart uniforms acting as hostesses. Alongside the displays there are areas where visitors can see demonstrations or take part in workshops. There is also a large traders' area where Satsuki of all sizes can be purchased.

Above all, the National Satsuki Festival is a competition. Winning top prizes at this event carries enormous prestige. Successful owners have photographs of themselves,

87

their Satsuki and their gardens featured in Satsuki Research magazine. Of course, everyone wants to win and the Japanese manage to avoid disappointing too many entrants by dividing the show into many classes and awarding lots of prizes. Indeed a first impression can be that almost every tree on display seems to have won a prize.

Satsuki Exhibition Classes

The Japanese National Satsuki Festival features all types of Satsuki and each entry is placed into one of the fifteen competition categories. These fifteen classes can be broadly divided into four groups:-

*An interested visitor contemplates some of the superb **Meika** Satsuki in the Tokyo Festival. The sheer size and physical impact of these plants is not easily appreciated from photographs.*

Meika

Meika translates as "Celebrated Flower" and the plants in *Meika* classes are judged on the quality of floral display. As well as perfection of blossoms, the judges also consider factors such as the variety of colour over the plant and the extent to which this reflects the full character of the variety involved.

In addition to the main *Meika* class, there is a special competition class for new varieties. This class is known as *Kiyogika*. This is open to the small number of new varieties which are awarded the Ministry of Agriculture Prize each year. This prize is the official seal of approval for any new varieties, without which they cannot be exhibited. There is also a class for recent winners of this prize, known as *Kihin* (Guest of Honour) Meika and another for these approved varieties introduced since 1979, known as *Saishin* (Up-to-Date) *Meika*.

Shinobazu pond in Ueno Park, Tokyo. The National Satsuki Festival is held on stands built around the edge of this pond.

Meiboku

The word **Meiboku** means an old tree of historical interest. **Meiboku** are the stunning bonsai masterpieces of the Satsuki world. Such trees form the core of a major Japanese exhibition. Satsuki bonsai which would fit into this category have rarely been seen in the West except in reproduction. Even more dramatic are those trees classed as **Shizen-Meiboku** (Natural Meiboku). These are ancient trees whose trunks have been growing since before the end of the **Meiji** era (1912). Both the **Meiboku** and **Shizen-Meiboku** categories are subdivided by size, with classes for trees over 45cm in height and for those between 30cm and 45cm.

One of the many traders' stands which were doing a brisk business during the Tokyo National Satsuki Exhibition

Shohin

The Japanese refer to very small or miniature bonsai as **Shohin**. This term is very familiar to western bonsai growers where it is generally translated as meaning "small goods". The word **Shohin** is indeed used in this context in everyday Japanese speech, though this is in fact a sort of Japanese pun. The original meaning of the **Kanji** for "**Shohin**" as used in bonsai is a small-scale artistic endeavour, such as a literary essay or a short piece of music.

Shohin Satsuki are divided into three classes by height, including a class for "Extraordinary Shohin" which are trees under 15cm. These are the miniature plants which most western growers would refer to as **Mame** (bean-sized) bonsai.

This very unusual Meika has both orange-red and purple selfs on the same plant.

Bonyo-Meiboku

Bonyo-Meiboku are Satsuki bonsai similar to the better commercial trees exported to the west. They are bonsai which have been trained from a very young age. While such trees would be judged as superb Satsuki bonsai if shown in the West, they are not considered to have achieved sufficient size, quality and substance to be classed as *Meiboku*.

Bonyo-Meiboku classes are divided by trunk diameter, which is measured at a height of 6cm above the root level. The smallest class is for trees with a diameter under 2cm, while to be eligible for the largest size class, the trunk must be over 6cm and under 8cm in diameter.

Few dedicated Satsuki shows have been held in the West outside of California (where they have long had a following).
This is part of a Satsuki show staged in a British Garden Centre.

Western Impressions of the Japanese Shows

In 1996 I visited both the Kanuma Satsuki Matsuri (Festival), followed by the National Exhibition in Tokyo.

Kanuma

For a visitor from Britain it was the sheer size of the plants which made the biggest impact, particularly the **Meika** trees which were up to 1.2 metres tall and 0.75 metres across! With the bonsai styles it was the large and beautiful trunks that stood out as being very different from anything seen in the West.

Something else which made a great impression over and above the plants themselves was the immaculate standard of

"Satsuki Girls" are very much a traditional feature of Japanese exhibitions. The author is seen here with two of the hostesses from the Tokyo Festival.

presentation. Major bonsai exhibitions in the West now achieve very high standards but my first sight of the Kanuma display brought home how much we could still improve. The display stands showed careful attention to detail in every aspect and great care had been taken to ensure that all possible distractions were screened from view.

The major prizewinning Satsuki bonsai on display in Kanuma were each presented in an individual tokonoma space nearly two and a half metres wide, with the tree on an antique display table and accompanied by its own exquisite accent planting.

One bench attracting a constant crowd was devoted to the year's new approved varieties. All of these were very attractive, though only one or two appeared particularly distinctive when

Attractive accent plantings are a notable feature of all Japanese Satsuki exhibitions.

94

compared to the many existing varieties. Considering that the current Japanese catalogues list nearly 1,000 varieties it is amazing to think that they still find a market for new ones. I was assured, however, that enthusiasts are still queuing up to get the latest plants in fashion.

Apart from the Satsuki themselves, the standard and variety of accompanying accent plantings was most striking. This is something that the Japanese have now raised into an independent art form in its own right, with its own monthly magazine.

Tokyo

Compared to the Kanuma Festival, the National Exhibition in Tokyo was very much bigger and had many more top quality trees on display; yet some aspects did not impress me as much. The sheer numbers of plants made it difficult to give each one the attention it deserved. The trees were crowded a little too close together and the hundreds-of-feet long display stands were functional rather than works of art in their own right. The difference between the two exhibitions is that the Kanuma Festival is aimed very much at the dedicated Satsuki lover, while the Tokyo show is designed to cater for a much wider audience. Entry to the National Exhibition is free and unobstructed. The display takes place on a public thoroughfare and many in the milling crowds are just passers-by taking a stroll through the park. Exhibition organisers in the West have become very concerned about the security of exhibits in recent years. It was striking that the Japanese felt quite comfortable about allowing the public free access to priceless bonsai with no security controls and little or no obvious stewarding.

chapter eight

Satsuki Growth and Pruning

The Satsuki Year

The Satsuki Growth and Care Cycle

When grown in a temperate climate with distinct seasons, a Satsuki plant exhibits a clearly defined cycle of growth. A clear understanding of this cycle is important if the correct maintenance and styling techniques are to be applied. The cycle set out here, is for a plant grown in the U.K., or in a similar northern hemisphere country.

January

General care

This is a quiet month in the Satsuki year. Plants will be in their winter quarters where they are protected from frost and wind. Satsuki need very little water at this time of year, but it is important to continue to check their needs as they can dry out. Watch out for forecasts of particularly severe weather and take extra precautions (e.g. insulating fleece) if heavy frosts are imminent. Remember that while large Satsuki bonsai can tolerate moderate frosts, young plants may be severely damaged in the same conditions. If your plants are kept in a greenhouse, be sure to ventilate it well on milder days to help prevent fungal diseases.

Satsuki shoot showing the dormant flower bud surrounded by the winter resting leaves.

Growth Pattern

The Satsuki plant is essentially dormant at this time of year. No activity can be observed in the shoots and buds. Root activity is minimal.

February

General Care

Conditions in this month are generally similar to January, though some Satsuki will show signs of growth in a mild year. Such early growth is very susceptible to frost damage so give extra protection. If frost should damage the new growing tips it should not be a great cause for worry. Such damage will not affect the health of a strong plant.

February is a good month to assess the future styling plans for Satsuki bonsai. At this time of year they have the minimal amount of foliage so it is easier to see the twig structure. If the weather is mild, light misting of the foliage can commence.

Growth Pattern

The growth buds that will form the new year's shoots can now be seen emerging from around the base of flower-buds which formed at the terminals of last summer's growth.

March

General Care

Satsuki begin to show strong signs of growth during this month. Plants should be fed from now on. It is particularly important to feed plants well at this time if they are expected to flower heavily, in order to build up their strength. If the weather is mild then give the plants more airy conditions but continue to watch out for frost. Late March is a good time to carry out detail wiring to refine the shape of established bonsai but do not carry out large amounts of wiring on a plant that is expected to flower.

Spring Re-potting

Satsuki in training can be repotted in mid-to-late March. This allows the plants the benefit of a full season of vegetative growth. Flowering should be restricted if spring re-potting is carried out and maximum growth will be obtained if all flower buds are removed.

Growth Pattern

The new shoots begin to grow around the flower-bud. From two to five shoots typically grow from each terminal.

During March the new shoots can be seen emerging from beneath the base of the flower-bud.

April

General Care

This is a month of very vigorous growth for Satsuki. Established bonsai of the stronger varieties may need pinching back twice during this month. The aim at this time of year is to prevent new growth from submerging the flower buds. Unwanted shoots such as those growing from the trunk, from branch junctions, growing downwards, etc. should be removed. Continue to feed the plants well throughout the month, with "little and often" being the best approach.

Plants should have their flower buds thinned out this month. If too many buds are left they will be squashed together and unable to open fully. One third or more of the buds are commonly removed from the trees shown in exhibitions.

Water requirements increase as the growth of the Satsuki speeds up.

Growth Pattern

On some of the stronger-growing varieties, such as Kaho, some new shoots may reach three or four centimetres in length by the end of this month. If shoots are not thinned and trimmed the flower buds become completely submerged beneath the new season's growth.

Summer leaves appear on the new shoots.

May

General Care

Flower buds should begin their final period of swelling in this month, though plants of some varieties, particularly when they have just been imported, may not enter the flowering phase until July.

Fertilizer should be withheld from flowering plants at this time as doing so helps to extend the flowering period. The flower buds should not be subjected to rain or spraying after they develop colour. Some form of overhead shelter is very useful at this time of year. If this also provides some shading and keeps the plant cool in hot weather, this will further help the quality of the display and to extend the life of the flowers.

The plant's demand for water increases dramatically as the flowers develop. It is essential that the soil be kept constantly moist at this time.

Growth Pattern

While the new season's shoots continue to extend, the most dramatic change in this month is the rapid swelling of the flower buds. Some varieties begin flowering from early May onwards. On most plants it will be found that one or two flowers become fully open about two weeks before the main flush.

Flower-buds swell rapidly and begin to show colour.

June

General Care

The beginning of June is the peak of the flowering season for most of the Satsuki varieties.

As flowering comes to an end, the busiest time of the year begins for the Satsuki hobbyist.

All the flower heads must be removed to prevent the formation of seeds which drain the plant's energy. Then follows the short period in which repotting, pruning and wiring are best carried out.

Plants which do not require repotting may be fed immediately after flowering is finished. Repotted plants should not be fed for three or four weeks.

Satsuki begin a second big flush of growth after flowering, and water demands remain high. Care must be taken not to overwater plants which have been repotted or heavily pruned, however, as these processes can dramatically cut down the plant's need for moisture.

The fifth moon of the Chinese lunar calendar (Sa-tsuki in old Japanese) is the time of flowering.

Growth Pattern

By the time of flowering, the new season's shoots on an untrained plant can be anything from 2cms up to 10cms, or even more. Shoot growth does slow down somewhat during the flowering period, however, as blossom development becomes the plants main priority.

July

General Care

Some Satsuki may still be flowering in this month but it is not advisable to let these late plants bloom for too long. This applies particularly if they need repotting, which should be carried out by the end of July at the very latest and earlier for plants of doubtful strength. If in any doubt about a plant's vigour (as indicated by the strength of the growing shoots, not by flower production), then always sacrifice this year's flowers in favour of the plant's long term health.

Satsuki branches thicken very rapidly at this time of year and any bonsai which have been wired should be checked every few days for the wire biting in. It is quite easy to miss the correct time for removing wire and the result can be a badly scarred tree.

No matter how attractive, flowers should be removed from plants by late July if re-potting is needed.

Continue to feed and water well in order to build up the plant's strength for the following year. Satsuki generally appreciate full sun conditions, except when in flower, but some light shading can be very beneficial if there are extended heatwave conditions.

Growth Pattern

Following flowering, the growth shoots put on a fresh spurt of growth, both thickening and extending.

On an untended plant, the flower slowly shrivels and the corolla, together with the stamens, part from the calyx. Many of these dead flower-parts fall to the ground but a lot of others are trapped among the foliage where they slowly decompose. If the flower has been fertilized, the ovaries now start to swell and the pedicel thickens and stiffens. Prior to this point the seed heads can be broken off, but after the pedicels strengthen they can only be removed by laboriously cutting each one.

Satsuki set considerable quantities of viable seed which germinates and grows readily. Producing plants from seed produced by your own bonsai is always fun but only one plant in many thousands is likely to have all the characteristics needed in a top-quality new variety.

After the flower falls, the developing seed pod will be left behind. This should be removed.

August

General Care

Major work such as repotting, pruning or heavy wiring should be avoided after the beginning of August. From this time on the plant should be allowed to build up its reserves for the winter. Also, the plant forms next year's flower buds at this time and any severe shock is likely to have a serious effect on next year's flowering performance.

Removal of unwanted shoots should still be carried out as necessary and plants may need some trimming and even a little detail wiring to keep them in shape.

Growth Pattern

Extension of the shoots continues but is now slowing. The buds which will form next year's flowers form at the tips of the current year's growth. Where shoots have been trimmed back earlier in the season, a second crop of shoots will also have extended by now.

The current season's shoots put on a fresh spurt of growth in August.

September

General care

Satsuki care in September is largely the same as in August. Growth is beginning slow down at this time and the plant's water requirements are less now than at the height of summer.

Growth Pattern

The main shoots have mostly stopped extending by this time of year and the new flower buds are clearly visible. Secondary growth is still extending. These secondary shoots also develop flower buds, provided that the trimming was carried out in good time. Late secondary shoots, or tertiary shoots, may or may not produce flower buds, depending on when they began to grow and on how long and mild the autumn is.

October

General Care

Satsuki produce two sets of leaves each year: the summer, or growing leaves and the winter, or resting leaves.

October is usually the month when the older, summer leaves on a Satsuki change colour and fall. In good years, where there are sunny days and cool, crisp nights, all the old leaves will change colour together, giving an attractive two-tone effect to the plant. In other years the leaves change colour and drop in dribs and drabs, and are merely untidy.

A last, light feed may be given early in this month before stopping fertilizer for the winter.

Growth Pattern

The distinguishing feature of the growth cycle at this time is the colouring and fall of the summer leaves. The remaining leaves, which support the plant over winter are clustered around the flower buds at the terminal of each shoot.

November

General Care

Satsuki care in this month is very dependent on the weather. If it remains fairly mild then the plants should be given as much fresh air as possible, but the grower must be alert to the possibility of frost and provide protection if necessary. Do not place the plants in their winter quarters too early, as this is likely to encourage soft growth.

December

General Care

Plants should be in their protected winter quarters this month, but remember to check if they need water. Water should be given in the mornings if the weather is cold, as the soil freezes more easily if watered just before dark.

Satsuki should still be given good ventilation whenever weather conditions allow. A watch must be kept for mildew and other fungal infections. Spray with a suitable fungicide if these are seen.

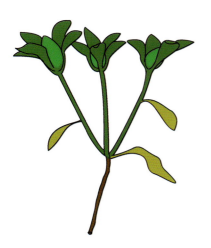

Through October, or November, the summer leaves change colour and fall, leaving only the flower-buds for next season surrounded by the winter, resting leaves.

The remainder of this chapter will examine the trimming and pruning processes in greater detail.

The Trimming Process

The routine trimming of new shoots is at the heart of styling a Satsuki. The basic techniques for doing this are very simple, though applying them to produce or maintain a Satsuki bonsai of the highest quality needs experience.

Removal of unwanted shoots

All new shoots growing where they are not wanted must be removed. Satsuki tend to send out shoots from anywhere on the plant, particularly when they are pinched back. Unwanted shoots include:

- those growing from the base of the trunk;
- those growing from the trunk itself;
- shoots growing from existing branch junctions;
- shoots growing downwards beneath the foliage pads.

This is a continual task and these shoots should be removed whenever they are seen.

Trimming and thinning before flowering

March

Satsuki should be checked at this time of year for any trimming jobs missed on last year's shoots. Any terminal with more than two shoots branching from the same point should be thinned.

April / May

It is desirable to control the new spring growth on trees destined for display, particularly on strong-growing plants. The new shoots can be thinned to two at each terminal and the remaining pair can be trimmed back to two leaves, if necessary. Where very strong shoots are disturbing the line of foliage pads it is sometimes desirable to remove all the new shoots from the offending terminals. These will be rapidly replaced by a fresh set of shoots.

On plants of more normal vigour, only odd shoots here and there will need removal or trimming back. Less vigorous and slower-growing varieties often require no trimming until after flowering.

Satsuki will produce buds on wood of any age. Cutting a vigorous plant back to old wood often results in an explosion of buds below the wound. This photograph was taken three weeks after pruning.

June / July - Trimming after flowering

The main period for trimming new growth is immediately after flowering. The growth is first thinned and then the remaining shoots are cut back to the required length.

Thinning the new shoots

Thin the new shoots growing at any one point to just two. Shears are not really needed for this task as the unwanted shoots can be broken off at the base by carefully bending them back towards the parent branch. The two shoots selected to keep are normally ones growing horizontally and spreading apart in a narrow "V".

Trimming back the new shoots

If growth is to be controlled the shoots that remain after thinning must be cut back. This is done using sharp scissors.

Shoot trimming options

The standard trimming process is to shorten the two shoots at each terminal to just two leaves. There are, however, many modifications that can be made to this procedure, depending on the requirements of the particular plant, or part of the plant.

One important variant concerns the apex of the plant. The apex of a Satsuki tends to be weaker than the other branches. For this reason, the apical twigs are often left with an extra leaf or two in order to encourage stronger growth if this is necessary.

Very strong, overgrown, or leggy areas of a bonsai require a minimum of new shoot extension. This can be achieved by cutting the shoots back close to the end of last year's growth. A new crop of secondary buds will then grow from the tip of last years shoot. This technique should also stimulate the production of new buds along the old twigs.

An even more extreme alternative which promotes even

Typical Satsuki branch before trimming. Several new shoots spring from the tip of last year's growth.

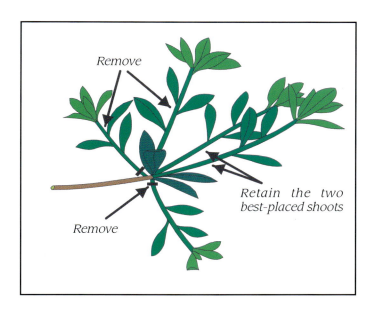

Stage one of the trimming process is to reduce shoots to two at each point. Scissors are not really necessary as the surplus shoots will snap off easily.

115

Shoots are next shortened to two new leaves.
This is the standard trimming procedure which gives optimum flowering in the following year, but results in steadily increasing size and density.

To prevent an increase in dimensions and to promote back-budding, this year's shoots can be cut back close to the base. Leaving a few leaves makes this process less stressful for the plant if vigour is not great.

stronger back budding is to prune back into last year's twigs, leaving no leaves at the tip. This is a technique which is widely used in the initial training of new bonsai but it should be practised on strong plants *only*. Beginners are advised always to leave at least a tiny bit of foliage on the tip of each twig.

Trimming back the current years growth results in the rapid production of secondary shoots. The required shoots are usually ones which spring from the leaf axils of the two remaining leaves. If the terminal is to divide in two, then just one bud from the base of each leaf should be allowed to develop. Many more buds than needed will often grow and these should be removed.

Carrying out the shoot trimming at the correct time is vital if the new secondary shoots are to mature in time to produce next years flower buds at their tips. Mid-July should be the latest target date for trimming in the U.K., though one can usually get away with this work up until the end of July on strong-growing, healthy plants.

For strong back-budding on older twigs and branches, cut back to last year's twigs. The resulting buds must then be thinned out.
Leaving tiny stubs from this year's growth is safer and gives quicker recovery. Even greater back-budding is achieved if the old twigs are shortened, but this process is not recommended for pot-bound plants which lack vigour.

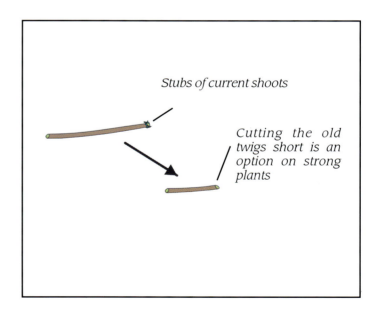

Pruning Satsuki

Pruning can be distinguished from trimming by the fact that it involves cutting into older wood. The current year's growth of twigs are greenish in colour, while older twigs and branches have brown bark. All cuts made into older wood should be sealed immediately to prevent die-back. It is best to use a proprietary bonsai wound-sealant for this purpose, but PVA glue will do. Cuts should be made with very sharp, clean tools.

When pruning Satsuki it is very important to remember that the top of the plant is less vigorous than the lower branches and must be pruned more gently.

Satsuki have the ability to re-bud strongly, even from old wood, but removal of many large branches is very stressful for the plant and can lead to die-back if not carried out correctly. Beginners are advised to gain some experience with Satsuki, or to seek further advice, before attempting to prune large branches.

Pruning large branches

In Japan many Satsuki bonsai are created by severe pruning of very large plants, which have been field grown for many years, or decades. This process involves sawing off very substantial branches and replacing them with new growth. Unfortunately, the sudden removal of very large branches can lead to problems. Japanese writers describe the difficulty as "sap withdrawal". When a small branch is

Severe pruning can rejuvenate an old neglected Satsuki. The bonsai opposite had not been trimmed for a number of year and all the inner shoots were dead.

The same tree is seen below after pruning back to the basic branch structure. Such severe treatment should only be carried out if the plant shows sufficient vigour. The level of vigour is only assesed by the strength of vegetative growth, not by flowering performance.

pruned, the Satsuki responds by throwing out new buds in the damaged area. When a large branch carrying a significant proportion of the plant's foliage is suddenly removed, however, the area below the cut may die back. Effectively, the Satsuki decides to abandon its growth efforts in the damaged area and concentrate all its energies elsewhere.

Sap withdrawal is not likely to be a problem with young plants or those which have been growing very vigorously. The size of branch which may give problems is very hard to specify. It might be dangerous to remove a branch of just one centimeter from a weak pot-bound bonsai but branches in excess of 5cms diameter can be removed quite safely from a vigorous Satsuki which has just been lifted from a growing bed.

Not all branches are equally prone to sap withdrawal. If the branch removed has live branches left both directly above and below it, then there is no danger, providing that the wound is properly sealed. The main danger branches are at the apex, which is always less vigorous anyway, and bottom branches which do not have other growth for some distance directly above them. In the case of these low branches, the sap paths often die back right down to the ground and the major roots below the branch also die.

When there is a worry of sap withdrawal occurring, the safe approach is to remove the large branch in stages. If all the foliage except for two or three leaves is removed from the branch, and all new buds which subsequently appear on it are rubbed off, then the branch can be removed with safety the following year. This is because the sap flow to that branch will already have slowed down to a trickle. It is also likely that new sprouts will have appeared around the base of the branch. A few of these new sprouts should be left growing because they will help maintain the sap flow when the branch is removed.

An alternative method used by Japanese growers for avoiding sap withdrawal is to saw a wedge out of the branch to about half of its diameter, at the point where it is to be removed. The amount of foliage on the branch is also reduced sharply. The hole left by removing the wedge is filled with cut-paste to prevent it drying out, and the branch is removed entirely the following spring. Again, the purpose is to cut down the flow of sap in stages rather than all at once.

The same tree pictured overleaf. This photograph was taken the following spring. The new shoots formed after pruning were then ready for detail wiring.

Aftercare

After any moderately severe pruning the plant should be given similar care to any other stressed plant. It should be placed in light shade and protected from any wind. Care must also be taken to avoid possible overwatering since stressed trees tend to take up much less water.

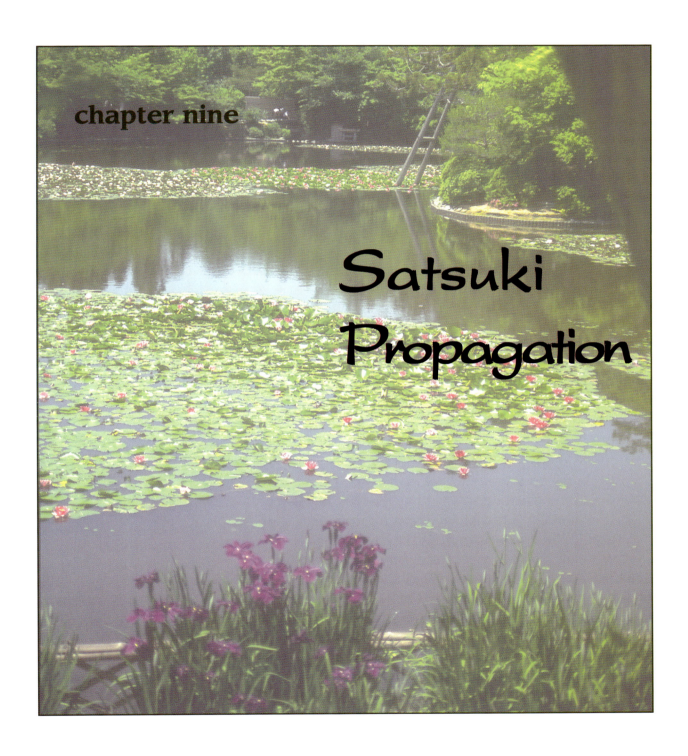

chapter nine

Satsuki Propagation

Satsuki Propagation

Propagation of Satsuki is not particularly difficult and plants can be produced by means of cuttings or air-layerings. Satsuki also grow readily from seed, but seedlings tend to revert back towards wild types and few are likely to bear flowers of Show-Satsuki quality.

Cuttings

Propagation of Satsuki by cuttings is very straightforward for anyone who has used this method for other woody plants. Softwood and hardwood cuttings can be used, though with differing degrees of difficulty.

Softwood Cuttings

This is the method used for the majority of commercial production. Shoots from the current year's growth are used and these root very rapidly under suitable conditions. The ideal piece of cutting material is around 5 to 7.5cm long and it should be as sturdy and firm as possible. In practice, material that is far short of this ideal can be used quite successfully. In particular, some of the slower growing varieties may only offer very short growths at the peak time for taking cuttings.

May is the best month for taking softwood cuttings. While soft cuttings will put out roots at any time, the later in the year they are taken, the harder it is to maintain them through the first winter. The keys to rapid rooting are warmth and high humidity. In Japan, cuttings are commonly rooted in low-roofed, very-high-humidity hot-houses. Automatic mist propagation is also ideal at a commercial scale. Amateurs can get good results by simply covering a deep seed tray with polythene and misting the cuttings once or twice a day. Good light is important but the cuttings will scorch in direct sun unless they are under an automatic mist system. Even under mist a small level of shading may be appropriate in very sunny weather.

Constituents of the soil used to insert the cuttings should be mildly acid and must drain well. The moisture retention of the medium must be adjusted to suit the type of watering regime. For a polythene-covered seed tray misted once each day, a 50 / 50 mix of coarse peat and pumice, or similar, will work well. For cuttings under heavy mist, a very much less retentive medium must be used. Japanese propagators use an extremely free-draining medium consisting of coarse (perhaps 4-6mm) grit, mixed with coarse Kanuma, over an even coarser drainage layer.

Cutting material should be placed in water as soon as it is removed from the plant. If cuttings are re-cut before insertion, this must be done with a very sharp clean blade. Cuts should be at right angles to the stem, not slanting. In practice, cuttings will usually root perfectly well if simply inserted as they broke off from the parent plant, but the resulting roots tend to be less even.

Hormone rooting powder may be useful but it is not essential. The lower leaves should be stripped away and the cuttings inserted

Satsuki cuttings at a Kanuma nursery.

vertically and closely spaced. The ideal depth of insertion is around 2cm. Try to ensure that no leaves are touching the soil as this causes rot problems.

Rooting can take anything from a few weeks to a couple of months or more, depending on the conditions. Plants which root slowly also tend to be less vigorous in future growth. Obtaining very rapid growth in the first year or two is very important. Slow growing plants and those which receive a check in their growth are much more susceptible to disease.

Begin fertilizing as soon as the majority of the cuttings have some roots (test with a gentle pull). Aim to get the maximum growth before the first winter. Cuttings taken early can often be repotted within 2 months of striking. Plants rooted later in the year and those showing less vigour are best left until the following spring.

It is essential that cuttings are kept frost free over the first winter. Many plants will never recover from a check at this stage.

In Japan, cuttings are commonly inserted into a very coarse medium, in deep polystyrene boxes.

Hardwood Cuttings

The typical hardwood cuttings used are the previous year's shoots taken in spring before new growth commences. These are a very reliable source of new plants and are treated in a similar fashion to softwood cuttings, though rooting takes much longer. The hardwood cuttings should be left for an entire year before potting on. Japanese nurseries begin taking this type of cutting in February.

Rooting Older Branches

Another type of hardwood propagation involves the rooting of old branches. This is a much more difficult procedure involving a lot of skill and luck, particularly where large material is involved. Japanese practice includes cutting the terminals back to just a few old leaves and wrapping the trunk with sphagnum moss. The rooting medium must be very open and watering demands great control. Even when this procedure is successful, the resulting plant often seems less vigorous than younger material but it is worth trying if an attractive branch is being pruned.

Air-Layering

This is the best method for rooting large branches and is quite reliable. The ideal piece of material is a large, well-shaped branch that is no longer required on the parent plant. A band of bark is removed immediately below where the roots are required and the wood beneath is scraped to remove all traces of cambium. The area is dusted with hormone rooting powder then wrapped with sphagnum moss then covered with polythene. The moss must be kept constantly damp without waterlogging. If this procedure is carried out in spring it is usually possible to cut the branch off in August. Should there be insufficient roots produced by then, the layer must be left until the following spring before being cut from the parent plant. Air-layerings must be protected from frost if left in place overwinter.

Propagating True-to-Type

The tendency to produce branch sports bearing different flowers is one of the great attractions of Satsuki. One mature plant can bear flowers with several different colours and patterns. Unfortunately, this variation causes problems when propagating by cuttings because shoots taken from some parts of the plant will not reproduce the variety correctly.

The typical multicoloured Satsuki which features *shibori*-patterned flowers will also bear white selfs and selfs of the contrast colour (usually pink or red). Often there will be both a darker and a lighter form of this contrast-colour self. In addition, the plant may also bear sokojiro or fukurin type blossoms.

When propagating from such a plant the likely outcomes are as follows:-

1) Branches bearing *shibori* flowers which are mostly white will generally yield the full colour range of the parent plant. Shoots from around *shibori* flowers which are heavily marked with the contrast colour are much less reliable.

2) Branches with white self flowers will usually yield plants of the parent type. Young plants are likely to bear white flowers only but variations will steadily increase as the plant matures. Eventually the problem is likely to be one of preventing the red-flowered branches from swamping the white ones.

3) Branches bearing selfs in the paler form of the contrast colour tend to give cuttings which show both paler- and darker-coloured selfs.

4) Shoots from branches bearing dark-coloured selfs will commonly give plants with flowers of that type only.

5) Shoots from branches with *sokojiro* or *fukurin* type flowers will generally produce flowers only of that pattern.

The variety **Kogetsu** is famed for the complexity of its flowering patterns. In order to obtain cuttings which will flower true-to-type, shoots should be taken from around white or lightly striped shibori flowers.

Shoots taken from branches which bear sokojiro flowers are likely to bear just the sokojiro pattern.

This flower shows the Janome or bulls-eye pattern. Shoots from around this flower would be unreliable.

Branches bearing only pure white or lightly striped flowers with no trace of any colour-ring patterns are the most reliable source for true-to-type cuttings.

Shoots from around fukurin flowers will tend to bear fukurin blooms.

Shoots from areas bearing coloured selfs generally bear just coloured selfs.

If you are uncertain as to which branches should be used for cutting-material, one fairly safe rule would be to choose those that seem to have the most typical flowers. e.g. on a **saizaki** variety, take cuttings only from areas with **saizaki** flowers. Branches reverting to full-petalled flowers are likely to yield plants with these full-petalled flowers only.

None of the above rules of thumb offer a guarantee that propagations will flower true to type. Fresh mutations within the plant material can occur, which can lead to different flower types; but the major problem is that each branch already carries a complex mixture of varied genetic material. The information which determines flower colour is carried within the cambium layer of the plant. Thus the colour of flowers on any new shoot is determined by the cambium material from which that shoot arises on the parent branch. In a variety with complex flower patterns, there will be different "types" of cambium around the circumference of the branches. On a branch with striped flowers, the stripes actually indicate which parts of the shoot's circumference carry which colour.

When propagating a saizaki variety such as Kinsai, it is important to avoid shoots bearing full, normal flowers.

It is important to keep a sense of proportion about these propagation problems. Young plants from an attractive Satsuki will themselves bear attractive flowers, even if they are not in the full colour range of the parent. There are many growers who prefer simple, single patterned plants to the excesses of some of the multicolour varieties.

Identifying Satsuki Branches

If cuttings are taken in early spring, before the parent plant flowers, there is clearly a problem in knowing which branches are the most reliable source of cutting material.

It is difficult, or impossible, to remember the flowering patterns from the previous year; there is also no practical way of recording the information on paper (though photographs are always a help). The solution is to mark the plant itself while it is in flower. In Japan the common practice is to mark important branches, such as those to be used for cuttings, by fixing a piece of wire loosely around them. It is possible to develop this into a more sophisticated system, by using coloured plastic bag ties (as used in the kitchen). Different branches can be marked with different coloured ties to represent different flower-types. Such a system would, in addition, require the maintenance of written records to provide a key to the colour codes.

If cuttings are required, but the plant was not marked when it flowered the previous year, clues to flower colour of various branches are often visible on the stems or leaves. On many plants, last year's shoots turn red or pink in winter if they bear red flowers. Leaves may also turn reddish on the same parts of the plant. On some varieties, a clear pattern of thin red stripes can be seen running along shoots which will bear striped shibori flowers. The position and spacing of these stripes around the circumference of the shoot is a good indication of the pattern a flower at the top of that shoot will have.

chapter ten

Creation of a Satsuki Bonsai

Creation of a Satsuki Bonsai

While the earliest bonsai were naturally dwarfed trees which were collected from nature and grown in containers, the vast majority of bonsai today are man-made creations. Satsuki bonsai are typically trained from their earliest days, even when they are not destined to be placed in a bonsai pot for many years, or even decades.

However grand the final result, the process of bonsai training is quite straightforward and works best when each stage is carried out as a separate and distinct process. No amount of technique will in itself produce a masterpiece. In the end, great bonsai are works of art and they reflect the artistic vision of their creator. Most people do possess far greater aesthetic skills than they ever employ, however, and gaining a knowledge of sound technique, plus experience, will enable growers to employ their artistic skills to the full.

This Satsuki of the variety "Hinotsukasa" was imported from Japan as a part-trained tree in a terracotta training pot. A move to a suitable bonsai pot and some branch refinement were all that was required to transform it into a very attractive bonsai.

Raw Material for Satsuki Bonsai

Sources of material for Satsuki bonsai are similar to those for other bonsai subjects:

a) A large field-grown plant can be cut down, and the stump used as the basis of a heavy-trunked bonsai.

b) A propagation can be grown-on until big enough to start bonsai training.

c) A part-trained, imported commercial bonsai can be purchased.

Large field-grown trunks are the favourite starting point for

Japanese Satsuki enthusiasts prefer to obtain to their trees as untrained trunks, just as they are lifted from the growing beds. Trunks at this stage, which allow complete freedom for the stylist's imagination, are rarely obtainable in the West.

135

serious enthusiasts in Japan. Unfortunately, material of this type is almost unobtainable in the West, because there are no available field-grown Satsuki to dig up and untrained stumps are rarely imported from Japan..

Growing from cuttings is relatively cheap and straightforward, providing that a parent plant is available or, alternatively, a source where young plants may be purchased.

The disadvantage of starting from a piece of young material is obviously the time it takes to produce a bonsai of any substantial size. This is an important consideration when the grower considers a big

This imported Satsuki has a well shaped trunk of high quality. The branches will need complete restyling before it is truly worthy of the term bonsai, however; a four or five year project.

impressive trunk to be the main attraction of Satsuki.

The final option, that of buying an imported tree, has the advantage of supplying a substantial piece of material to work with immediately. The downside of this approach being the considerable cost involved. Satsuki are expensive in Japan and this is reflected in the prices of imported trees. In the case of large trees with good-quality trunks, the supply also tends to be very limited and a very large proportion of the available trees has tended to be of the varieties **Kaho** or **Gyoten**. This has placed very strong restrictions on anyone with the ambition to build a good collection of different varieties, though the choice of imported varieties is gradually improving.

A purchased import will generally require a lot of work before it can be considered a fine bonsai, but results do not take long to achieve if care is taken to purchase a suitable trunk. This is the key to buying a good bonsai of any kind. Providing that the trunk is of good quality, all the branches, twigs, etc. can be developed in a relatively short time. A poor trunk, however, never gets any better.

*A large proportion of the bigger Satsuki imported into Europe in recent years have of the variety **Kaho** and its pink sport, **Gyoten**.*

Production of a Satsuki bonsai from raw material

Development of young plants

The vast majority of Satsuki begin life as cuttings. Since a substantial trunk is a crucial feature in most styles of bonsai, starting from a cutting is obviously a long-term project. Exactly how long it takes to produce something worthy of the term bonsai depends on many factors. Apart from the obvious question of the size and trunk diameter required, the particular variety chosen and the skill and knowledge of the grower make a great deal of difference to the speed at which a plant can be developed.

It is quite feasible to produce an attractive small bonsai in the 20-25 cms height range and with a trunk diameter of between 1 and 2cms in about six years. Growers with ambitions to produce large bonsai with trunk diameters in the 10 cms plus range need to accept that they are taking on a thirty- to forty-year project!

Training trees from cuttings

Satsuki produce two quite distinct types of growing shoot and an understanding this is important if rapid trunk development is to be obtained. Mature flowering shoots tend to be short and with leaves all along their length. Mature shoots normally spring from the tips of last year's growth and they will develop flower-buds at their terminals in midsummer. The other type of new growth is the juvenile, or sprout-type growth which the plant uses to form major new branches. Sprouts are much thicker and sturdier than the flowering shoots. They rapidly elongate to several inches and often bear leaves only near the tips. Sprouts can arise from any part of the plant, particularly at the base of the trunk, at branch junctions and around old pruning scars.

Finished bonsai require adult flowering growth, but when a young Satsuki is being grown on, it is juvenile, "sprout" type growth that needs to be encouraged. The rapid development of many sprouts is what produces the trunk thickening.

If left to its own devices, a typical Satsuki plant of three or four years old would have half a dozen or more trunks emerging from the ground. The height of such a plant is unlikely to be more than 25cm-30cm and, in the case of dwarf varieties, might be only 10cm.

The height reached and the growth habit displayed by a young plant is to some extent determined by the type of parent material from which the cutting was taken. If the cutting has been taken from a flowering branch, then the new plant will produce very compact growth and will probably flower in the year following rooting. If the cutting has come from a sprout, the plant will grow much faster but will take longer to flower. These two points are directly related. Whenever a Satsuki shoot develops flower buds, it ceases any attempt to increase in height. The multiple-trunk form of young Satsuki results from the fact that strong growth of each shoot stops as it forms flower buds, and the growth energy is redirected to the production of new sprouts from the base of the plant. The plant therefore develops its natural form as a wide, low, ground-hugging bush.

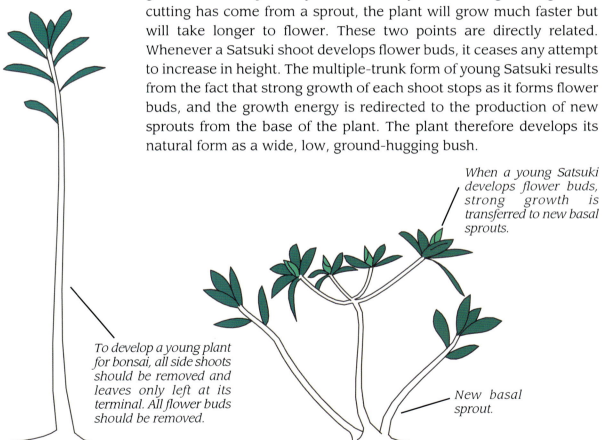

When a young Satsuki develops flower buds, strong growth is transferred to new basal sprouts.

To develop a young plant for bonsai, all side shoots should be removed and leaves only left at its terminal. All flower buds should be removed.

New basal sprout.

Removal of Flower Buds

If a young plant is producing flower buds which are interfering with growth, it is desirable to remove these. The buds can be removed at any time from late autumn onwards if they are large enough to handle. Varieties which produce large flower buds before winter can be bud-stripped several weeks before those bearing small buds. This is a delicate and time-consuming operation which is best carried out using tweezers, particularly for small buds. The new growth buds sprout from immediately below the flower bud and great care must be taken not to damage these new growth points. It will be found that buds on some varieties break away easily, while others are difficult. Where buds resist breaking off, it is very easy to damage the plant itself.

In Japan, high quality Satsuki trunks are commonly produced in deep growing beds which are given polythene tunnel protection in winter.

Initial Trunk-Shaping

The initial wire-shaping of the trunk can be carried out after two to four years of growth, depending on the size of the plant and how big a final bonsai is planned. If a very small bonsai is planned then shaping should be done as soon as possible. For large bonsai it is best to let the plant make a good height first. Earlier shaping is easier because the young trunk is more flexible. Japanese commercial practice is to apply this trunk wire in the autumn, but remember that frost protection is essential for wired trees. An advantage of wiring at this time is that the plants have lower sap levels and consequently are not quite so brittle. They are also less susceptible to having the bark

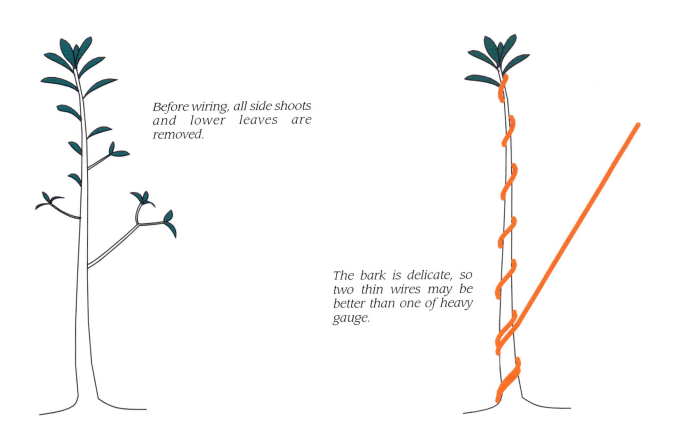

Before wiring, all side shoots and lower leaves are removed.

The bark is delicate, so two thin wires may be better than one of heavy gauge.

scraped off. Initial wiring can also be done in spring or early summer, but great care must be taken to observe the plants for signs of the wire biting in because this happens extremely quickly on young plants during the main growing season.

The wire for bending the trunk should be pushed firmly into the soil, taking care not to damage any potential surface roots. (Judicious scraping away of the soil is recommended before inserting the wire.) As when wiring any bonsai, the stiffness of the wire must match the stiffness of the branch being bent. Given the brittle nature of Satsuki and their delicate bark, it is often easier and safer to apply two thinner wires rather than one thick one.

It is important to think in terms of the scale of the final bonsai when forming the trunk curves.
At this stage the bends should be exaggerated a little, for they will become less extreme as the trunk thickens.

After applying the wire, it is best to picture the desired trunk shape before commencing any bending. Once the trunk has thickened it will be impossible to change the shape, so this one task may be the most important in establishing the future quality of the plant as a bonsai.

Deciding how many bends to put in the trunk and how severe these should be, is quite difficult. The grower needs a clear idea of the final dimensions the plant will have as a bonsai, and what sort of trunk diameter it will be grown on to before beginning bonsai training. Competence in bonsai styling cannot be learned by reading books. The best route to attaining the skills is through practice combined with the careful study of as many good bonsai as possible.

Many Satsuki imported from Japan are poor-quality examples of the Repeated "S" style. These often have grotesquely exaggerated and artificial-looking curves. This type of extreme bending is to be avoided at all costs. On the other hand, it is important to remember that bends will become much less severe as the trunk thickens. When trunks are grown on to very large dimensions, curves that once looked highly exaggerated can almost disappear.

The other thing to avoid when shaping trunks, is the perfect textbook Informal Upright shape. This appears as a diagram in many bonsai books, but it should be seen as an illustration of basic styling principles, not something to be copied exactly. - Real trees are much more unpredictable and eccentric.

The aim of all trunk development work should be to arrive at a tree which looks both natural and impressive.

Trunk development

Wire should be left on the trunk until it is just starting to bite. The young tree will then be set in its new shape and the programme of trunk-fattening can begin. In Japan, commercial quality trees are thickened in fields or nursery beds, while high quality trees are often thickened using deep beds inside poly-tunnels. The best approach for a British grower would probably be to plant the young tree in a large pot or growing box, unless it is possible to construct a suitable bed in a greenhouse.

The young trunk is planted out in a growing bed.

When planting out the young trunk, the root system should be evened out, and any high roots or roots which cross over others should be removed. This will give the plant a good start towards an attractive root system. After this root-pruning, the tall leggy trunk may need staking until it becomes established. From this point on, the aim is to take advantage of the Satsuki habit of sending out strong sprout growth as a response to pruning. Every two years or so, all the branches should be pruned back very hard and this stimulates new sprouts from all over the trunk. Sprouts growing at or below soil level should be removed frequently. The only regular requirements for the plant during this process are water and fertilizer plus an occasional pesticide spray.

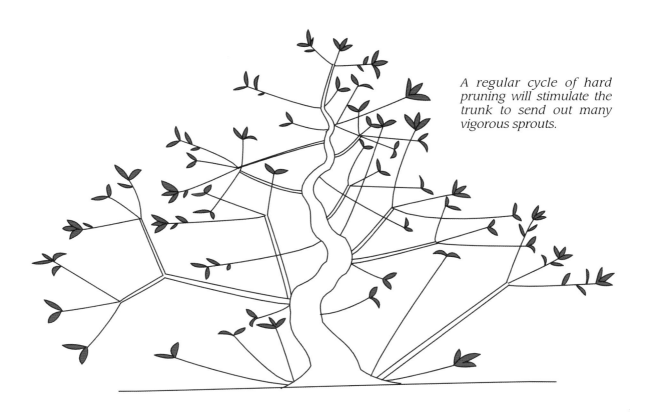

A regular cycle of hard pruning will stimulate the trunk to send out many vigorous sprouts.

The move to a training pot

The time will come when the Satsuki trunk has reached a suitable size to begin its bonsai training. There is no correct point at which training should begin, it is often the impatience of the grower which determines how long the tree is allowed to fatten. The tree is then lifted from the growing bed and begins its life in a container. This is the stage at which most Japanese enthusiasts like to buy their trees. Japanese Satsuki magazines are crammed with advertisements showing photographs of untrained trunks for sale at the just-lifted-from-the-ground stage. Unfortunately, plants at this interesting stage are rarely available for sale in the West, because trees exported from Japan have nearly always had some initial branch training.

The trunk should be lifted from the bed with a generous root-ball. Take care to ensure that the roots do not dry out while you carry out work on the top of the plant.

The work on the trunk consists of cutting it down to the required height and removing any significant branches which will not be part of the final design. If there are any small shoots which have potential for development as branches, these are left on with a minimal amount of foliage. A few other small shoots may be left at the apex, or around major wounds. The foliage on these small growths will help to sustain sap flow while the trunk re-buds.

When the trunk has the required dimensions, all the branches are cut off. The roots are washed clean of soil and pruned. The trunk is planted in a training pot to begin its styling.

Creating Meika-Type Plants

Most Satsuki trained in Japan today are still styled in a "Repeated-S" form. Nearly all of the Informal Upright style trees being developed in Japan today started out as Repeated-S trunks which were modified by pruning and further fattening. Trees in "Repeated-S" and "Repeated-Z" styles have been the standard Japanese commercial output for much of this century, though the fashion for the most extreme and grotesquely exaggerated curves has gradually waned. This highly artificial approach to shaping trunks has proved to be well suited for the production of **Meika**-type show plants. When branches are grown from the outsides of the bends, a well-bulked bush is quickly created that provides the structure for an impressive display of flowers. The trunk bends help to offset the position of branches, thus preventing them from shading one another too much.

Creating **Meika**-type plants for floral display follows exactly the same process as described below for bonsai. The big difference is that there is no waiting for a thick trunk to develop. With Meika the process is simply to achieve the desired height as quickly as possible, then bend to shape. For very large plants this process of growing-on then wiring may have to be repeated. When the required trunk height is achieved the plant can be transferred to a training pot and the branch development can begin.

As stated in an earlier chapter, there is a danger of sap withdrawal if large branches are suddenly removed from any but the most vigorous plants. If in doubt, it is safer to remove the branch in stages. All wounds on the trunk must be carefully sealed.

The next stage is to prepare the roots for potting. A strong jet of water should be used to remove all the soil from the roots. The roots themselves are then cut back to the size and shape of the pot. This first training pot will probably have to be considerably larger than the final choice of container, but Satsuki have well-branched root systems which can be reduced very hard. Particular care should be taken to even out the top of the root system. All crossing roots should be removed, or straightened and pegged in place. The aim is to accentuate the natural Satsuki trunk flare by leaving only those surface roots which slope downwards and outwards at a suitable angle. Any twisted or eccentric knuckle-roots which break this line down into the soil should be removed, unless, of course, they are large enough and interesting enough to really form a primary feature of the bonsai design.

After the initial branch structure is formed, the new bonsai-in-training is planted in a bonsai pot.

Potting up the new bonsai follows standard practice, but these newly potted trees should always be tied or wired into the container. This keeps them stable until new fine feeder roots can form. The soil mix used should be very porous. Whether Kanuma, or a humus-based compost is used, it should be sieved and the fines discarded. Adding chopped sphagnum moss to Kanuma is very

Producing Trunks by the Chop-and-Grow Method

The formation of large, well tapered trunks with many other bonsai species is achieved by a process known as chop-and-grow. This involves allowing a plant a period of unlimited growth, after which the trunk is cut down very low and a new leader developed from a small side shoot. The side shoot is wired into position as a new apex and the process is repeated. The cycle of growing and chopping back continues, cutting to a higher point on the trunk each time, until suitable thickness and taper are achieved. Branch development and bonsai training then follow.

Western enthusiasts repeatedly ask why they should not use this familiar method to produce Satsuki trunks. Satsuki lack the apical dominance which is a key feature of species developed in this way. Pruning a Satsuki trunk down to a low level produces an explosion of new growth, but this is all concentrated around the base of the trunk. Growth in the apical area tends to be much less vigorous and in extreme cases die-back may occur.

The standard Japanese method of producing Satsuki trunks, involving the development of a tall thin plant then fattening by use of side shoots, has been tested and proved over many decades and westerners are highly unlikely to achieve comparable results using different approaches.

The chop-and-grow approach does have one possible application for Satsuki, however. This type of approach is used in Japan for the production of Mame and small Shohin bonsai, up to a height of perhaps 15cm to 20cm. Chops on a plant of this size are in scale with the natural Satsuki growth habit. In fact at this size range it becomes difficult to distinguish the two approaches, because fattening shoots rapidly grow to equal the main trunk diameter.

important when severe root pruning is carried out as it helps the production of new roots. A thick layer of sphagnum (or even coarse peat, if sphagnum is not available) should be placed over the soil surface to maintain the humidity. This layer of moss should be removed when new white roots are seen starting to grow up into it.

The move from growing bed to pot is commonly undertaken in spring. The tree is then allowed a recovery period and fed to encourage a crop of strong new shoots.

Initial branch selection

The shoots which will be used to form the basic branch structure of the new bonsai should not be chosen until the plant has an abundant head of healthy new growth. This may take only a few months in some cases, while others may require a full year of recovery. All the new shoots which will not form part of the final design are then eliminated and those selected for branches are wired into position. This is another of the crucial stages in a bonsai's development. The angle at which the branches spring from the trunk is determined now, and this is one of the main determinants of the tree's style. Once the branches

Refinement of the twig structure is the last stage in bonsai development. This is an ongoing process.

have grown and set into position, this basic branch angle can be altered only by removing all these branches and starting again.

The wire on the new branches must be checked very regularly and removed in good time. The young branches should be allowed to lengthen without a check, unless one particular part of the plant, usually the apex, is showing much less vigour than the rest. In that case the strongest growths should be cut back to allow the weaker parts to catch up a little.

The whole process of selection, thinning out and wiring should be repeated the following spring, and it will often be possible to select and wire again by midsummer. In this way the new branch-pads are quickly built up. By the end of the second year the tree should be starting to look like a genuine bonsai, though the foliage pads will probably still be much too small in proportion to the trunk.

Silk Purse from a Sow's Ear?

Many growers despair of ever having good quality Satsuki trunks to style. The photo sequence on these pages shows another development from an untrained trunk through to the early stages of bonsai training. In this case, however, the material was far from ideal, having received no trunk shaping in its early years. Most bonsai growers would reject such raw material as impossible for bonsai work.

This plant will never develop into a high quality bonsai but can with patient development become a very pleasant tree which can provide a stunning display during the flowering period.

*Above: This plant of the variety **Hikarugenji**, had a very ugly trunk which offered little potential as a bonsai.*

After severe pruning, the remaining shoots were wired into place. The lack of curves in the trunk dictates the development of heavy foliage masses which will disguise the poor shape.

Nine months later, the small shoots have produced a lot of new foliage. This must in turn be thinned and wired to form the basis of the future branch pads.

One year later the tree continues to make progress. As the foliage mass extends, attention will be drawn away from the dull trunk. Care must be taken to ensure that the foliage retains distinct branch lines and does not degenerate into a simple "mop" shape.

Basic Satsuki Requirements

Soil

Satsuki are "lime-hating" ericaceous plants which require an acid soil to thrive. A pH range from 4.5 to just over 6.0 is tolerated. Providing that lime levels are low, however, there is no need for the soil to be strongly acid. A pH of 6.0 will be found quite adequate. If the soil mix satisfies this requirement, then there is a lot of flexibility regarding the actual ingredients used.

The important physical characteristics of the potting medium are that it should be well aerated and that it should drain freely while still retaining a moderately high level of moisture. Adequate pore space is very important because, although Satsuki roots require constant even dampness, they also require the presence of air in order to function. Azaleas rapidly succumb to root rot in waterlogged soils.

Finished bonsai are subject to regular trimming and are therefore unable to grow with the same vigour as a plant allowed unrestrained growth. For a Satsuki in this low vigour situation the provision of a perfect soil mix is much more critical.

In the West, azalea potting mixtures have traditionally been based on peat: in Japan, the acid subsoil known as **Kanuma-tsuchi** forms the principal potting ingredient. This material offers the desired acidity and moisture retention, with an open granular structure which resists breakdown to dust.

Kanuma has a poor reputation with some British bonsai enthusiasts. This is generally

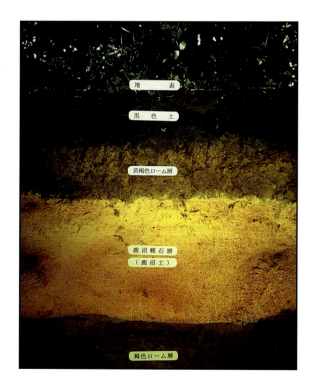

This photo in a Japanese exhibition shows a section through the soil in the Kanuma area. The yellow band is the Kanuma-tsuchi.

because their experience of the material has been limited to working with imported trees which are several years overdue for repotting. In that situation, the Satsuki roots grow through every **Kanuma** particle, binding them together into something resembling a "cream-coloured concrete block". Repotting a tree in this state can be a very frustrating and time-consuming operation. If bonsai are repotted in good time, however, **Kanuma** is a very pleasant material to use. If available, it is an excellent choice for potting finished bonsai, despite its high cost.

While **Kanuma** can be used on its own for bonsai, in Japan it is mixed with anything up to 50% of chopped sphagnum moss. The higher percentages of moss are used following severe root disturbance. In addition to supplying additional moisture retention, sphagnum also seems to play a part in promoting fresh root growth. The addition of sphagnum is by no means essential when repotting established plants in good condition. Some Japanese experts even advise against its use in this case.

Other soil mixes quoted by Japanese sources include various mixtures of **Kanuma**, peat, grit and **Akadama**; e.g. 50% **Kanuma** and the remaining 50% split evenly among the other ingredients.

A good starting point for a potting compost using western ingredients would be 50% long-fibred coarse peat (or a good peat substitute), 30% pumice or calcined clay (e.g. "Biosorb") and 20% grit. If available, up to 50% percent **Kanuma** could be added to this mix.

For young pre-bonsai plants putting on vigorous growth, a mix containing more humus will work well; e.g. 75% long-fibred peat (or good peat substitute) and 25% pumice. **Kanuma** does not seem to offer a particular advantage for young plants being rapidly grown on. I have found that young cuttings consistently put on more growth in a peat-based mix than in **Kanuma**.

Water

Given the "lime-hating" character of azaleas, they are much easier to maintain if a supply of soft, acid water is readily available. In areas with hard tap water, growers will probably have to consider a means of collecting rainwater. Rainwater is by far the best choice during the winter months (when the plants need less water anyway). During the summer months there can be a problem in collecting enough fresh rainwater. In this case tap water may be used with the addition of a suitable soil-acidifier. The most suitable product available is the combined acidifier and fertilizer named "Miracid" (produced by Zeneca in Europe). This is obtainable from most good Garden Centres. A small amount of Miracid is added to the tap water before use. Establishing the correct amount requires experimentation. If the leaves begin to look pale and yellowish or reddish then the amount should be increased. If they become a very dark blackish-green then the amount must be reduced.

Another acidifier quoted by growers in hard water areas is phosphoric acid. If you can obtain phosphoric acid diluted to 10% with water, then an occasional addition of this (one teaspoon per gallon of water) will re-establish the required acidity levels.

Fertilizer

Satsuki are derived from a group of plants which are adapted to living on very poor soils. This means that their fertilizer requirements are a little different from those of many other plants. The supply of a correctly balanced mixture of all the different trace elements is much more important than giving large quantities of Nitrogen, Phosphorus or Potash.

Satsuki can be a little choosy about the type of fertilizer used. It is best to stick to feeds recommended for ericaceous plants such as heathers, rhododendrons, etc. and to test unknown fertilizers carefully, particularly before applying at high strengths. The excellent liquid feed and soil-acidifier "Miracid" is as good as any of the generally available products.

Japanese growers use organic feeds for their Satsuki bonsai. Imported organic "bonsai" fertilizers vary in quality but good products such as "Biogold" give superb results. These Japanese fertilizers are very expensive and tend to be used mainly for high-quality show specimens. While they are by no means essential, they are a great aid to maintaining plants in peak show condition.

Feed should be given throughout the growing season, except for a period from early May until after flowering. Some growers consider a feed of 0-10-10 fertilizer is desirable in late summer. This is said to be helpful for flower bud development, but I have never found it essential. Azalea roots remain slightly active throughout the winter and feeding should be continued quite late into the autumn. A final feed should be given when the spring leaves change colour.

Satsuki require chelated trace elements as part of their feeding programme. If these are not included in the fertilizers used, they should be supplied separately in the form of a spring feed of "Sequestrene" or similar product.

Careful fertilizing is needed if plants are to flower well on a regular basis.

Position

Satsuki require a light, airy situation, in a sheltered spot out of doors, or in a cool, well ventilated conservatory or greenhouse. Full sun is tolerated though a degree of shading can make care much easier in very hot conditions.

During the flowering period, plants should be placed in a shaded position. They still require some sunlight, however, and the ideal position would allow the plants just a few hours of early morning sun. Flowering plants should also be positioned under some type of cover which prevents rain from falling on the flowers.

Placing Satsuki in a shaded position during the flowering period gives a longer lasting display.

Satsuki pests

Azaleas are relatively free of insect pest problems. Although a number of exotic azalea-specific pests are listed in Galle's monograph, the most common foliage infestations in the U.K. are likely to be aphids and the odd caterpillar. These are easily dealt with using proprietary insecticides.

Red Spider Mite is occasionally mentioned as a problem, but this is generally a pest which thrives in dry greenhouse conditions, rather than the more humid air preferred by Satsuki. Red spider mite can be both difficult to detect and difficult to eliminate. Proprietary chemicals recommended for this pest should be used, but repeated treatments may be necessary to eradicate an infestation.

Vine Weevil is currently the insect pest most feared by growers of Satsuki (and all other bonsai). The adults do not generally cause severe damage, though they do chew Satsuki foliage. It is the soilborne vine weevil grub which causes potentially fatal damage to plant roots. These grubs can destroy the root system - of young plants in particular - before the grower is even aware there is a problem.

The vine weevil is extremely resistant to most insecticides. Gamma BHC powder mixed into the compost gives a good measure of control, however. Another option is to treat all the plants in a collection with parasitic nematodes which destroy the grubs. Other, more effective, chemical treatments are now becoming available to the horticultural trade, but are not on sale to the general public due to their high toxicity.

Yet another option for vine weevil control relies on the fact that the adults cannot fly. If Satsuki are kept isolated from the ground on raised benches, it is possible to apply bands of grease around all the legs of these benches, on which the adults can be trapped and killed. With a little thought, all new purchases could be given a separate, grease-protected quarantine bench to keep any emerging weevils isolated.

Fungal diseases

Root-rot

The most serious disease problem encountered by Satsuki growers is fungal root rot . The first symptoms to be observed are usually the wilting and dropping of a plant's leaves, but the damage has actually occurred at the fine feeder roots. If the roots are examined they will appear brown rather than a healthy white colour.

Basic hygiene measures should be maintained at all times in order to prevent a build-up of infection, but these organisms are extremely widespread, attacking thousands of different plant types and able to survive for very long periods without a host.

High soil-moisture levels are the principal factor in triggering an attack of root rot, as the fungal spores require a film of free water in order to move through the soil. Use of a well-drained compost and careful control of water are thus major factors in the prevention of this disease. The other key procedure is a regular preventative spraying regime, using a suitable systemic fungicide.

Foliage diseases

The other regularly encountered fungal problems are likely to be powdery-mildew-type infections of the foliage, and azalea gall.

Mildews are almost always a symptom of poor ventilation. In general, they are only encountered when Satsuki are crowded together in winter quarters where they are surrounded by still, damp air. Mildews are easily controlled by systemic sprays and an improvement in environmental conditions.

Azalea gall is a disfiguring disease where leaves, or other parts of the plant, swell into large hard lumps. Fortunately, this disease is rarely a serious threat to the plant's health. The fungus is spread only externally, not through the plant tissues. Removal and disposal of galls, preferably by burning, before they reach the infective, powdery stage can prevent its spread. Certain Satsuki varieties seem much more prone than others to this problem and its incidence varies greatly from year to year. Humid, shady conditions are a factor in encouraging the disease, and a move to a more open airy position is often all that is required to effect a cure. Fungicidal sprays are also fairly effective, particularly the traditional copper-based sprays..

Winter Protection

Satsuki azaleas are quite hardy when grown in the open ground on the South coast of England. In areas which are subject to hard frosts, however, they may be subject to damage in severe weather if they are not given protection. This applies even more when plants are grown in containers.

Many Satsuki are grown commercially in Japan using growing tunnels to provide winter protection.

The polythene covers are often removed from the tunnels during the summer months.

In general, the bigger and the more mature a plant is, the better it will stand up to cold weather. Young material, up to two or three years of age, should be regarded as tender. Frost damage on these small plants usually takes the form of the bark splitting away from the wood. Such splits are easily recognised and should be sealed with *Kiyonal*, "Cut-paste", or some similar product. If the damage is not too severe, plants will recover, though growth may remain weak for a considerable period.

Large Satsuki will usually stand several degrees of frost for a short time, but the degree of hardiness seems to vary with the particular variety. The general health and vigour of the individual plant almost certainly play a part as well.

If a Satsuki is a treasured possession, it would be foolish not to give it a little protection in frosty weather. In all but the most severe frosts, a cold greenhouse will suffice. For young cuttings or weak trees, an additional covering with insulating fleece might also be needed. This material would also be useful as a more general protective covering during unusually prolonged or heavy frosts. The rare British winter which is severe enough to require even better frost protection than this is almost certainly going to damage other bonsai species as well. On such occasions, some form of background heating for the greenhouse could be a life-saver, but this might only be needed once in every seven to ten years in most parts of Britain.

If a grower does not have access to a greenhouse, Satsuki can be protected by placing them in a garage or shed for a day or two during a cold snap. If protection is needed for longer periods, then adequate light must be supplied. Another option would be to bring the Satsuki into a cool room within the house (e.g. an unheated porch).

The above paragraphs refer to British conditions. Satsuki enthusiasts in other parts of the world keep plants in climates with much more severe winters. In such circumstances, the grower has to devise much more efficient frost protection for overwintering.

chapter eleven

Popular Satsuki Varieties

Variety Names

Until recently, the vast majority of Satsuki that found their way to Europe had no accompanying variety name. Unfortunately, this is still true for most of the lower-priced, commercial plants, but at least some importers are now making a serious effort to obtain names for the plants they buy. Strangely, the Japanese themselves have been very slow to realise that foreigners would be interested in knowing the Japanese names for their plants, or indeed that Satsuki growing could ever become a serious hobby outside Japan.

Growers interested in building a collection of correctly named varieties have thus faced considerable problems. The range of correctly named plants is now growing steadily, though some varieties are having to be discarded from the list when it becomes clear that names attributed to them were incorrect.

Given the problems in propagating true-to-type, mentioned in Chapter 5, many Satsuki varieties can rapidly lose some of their essential characteristics if propagation is not carried out with great care. One source of named plants has been California, where Satsuki growing has a longer history. Unfortunately, some of the plants from California appear quite distinct from varieties with the same name in Japan.

Individual cuttings taken from a correctly identified plant may not show all the characteristics of the parent. Such plants are often referred to in the USA as the "#2" version of the variety. These are often very desirable plants in themselves but should ideally not be used for further propagation (see the illustration of the all-pink *Dai-Seiko* on page 90).

In a few cases, where no better alternative is available, a rare plant which lacks the full colour range of the true variety has been adopted as a stock plant. This should really be just a stopgap measure, until the correct stock can be obtained. The variety *Gyokurei* illustrated in this chapter fits in this category.

This chapter illustrates and describes some of the most popular Satsuki currently available in the West. This is the first section of its kind in English and should be a valuable reference for enthusiasts who have so far have had to rely on Japanese catalogues.

Abbreviations used in this chapter - (G.) signifies that the variety is described by Galle in his monograph on azaleas. (T.S. page ***) identifies the page number in the current Japanese Tochinoha Shobo dictionary of Satsuki varieties.

Unamed Variety

This very attractive Satsuki is typical of the bonsai that arrive in Europe with no variety name. No-one has been able to identify it, but it is so beautiful I have given it a code number - S932.

Asahi-no-Hikari
[The Light of Dawn]

(G.) (T.S. page 731)

Sport of Eikan

Pale pink fading to white, often with deeper pink margins. Many flowers with deeper pink sectors. Medium-large (6.5cm-7.5cm) flowers with round, ruffled lobes. Late flowering.
This variety is vigorous and is considered in Japan to be one of the best suited to rapid trunk thickening.

Bunka
[Cultured]

(G.) (T.S. page 135)

Kyokkonishiki X Seidai seedling from early Taisho era. (N.B. Galle states that this is a seedling of Yata-no-Kagami.)

Soft pale pink, shading to whitish-pink in centre. Medium-large (6cm-7cm) flowers with rounded petals. Slow to medium speed growth with spreading habit.

Chiyo-no-Homare
[Glory of a Thousand Years]

(G) (T.S. page 304)

Seedling of Tomari-Hime.

Large (8cm), full, white flowers with varied amounts of striping and banding in pale or deep orange-pink. Where background is orange, blotch is deep orange. Growth is medium to vigorous with an upright habit.

Chigosugata
[Celestial child figure]

(G) (T.S. page 128)

Hogetsu X Taihei

White centre with wide border of rose or coral pink. Medium-large flower (6cm-7cm) with round, overlapping wavy petals. Vigorous.

Chojuho
[Treasure of Longevity]

(G) (T.S. page 95)

Seedling originating in the Taisho era (1912-1926). Parentage unknown.

Very unusual. Flowers open deep red and fade through orange then greenish to light brown. Flowers will remain on plant until winter. Small flowers with narrow strap like lobes, (2.5cm-3.5cm) with very prominent stamens. Vigorous spreading growth.

Dai-Seiko
[Great Starlight]

(G) (T.S. page 285)

Sport of Gobi Nishiki

White with occasional stripes of deep pink, varying to deep pink selfs with white border. Wide-spaced pointed petals turned back at ends, (6cm-7.5cm). Slow compact habit.

Gyokurei
[Gem]

(G) (T.S. page 201)

Kaho X Mme. Moreux seedling.

Double flower (6cm-7.5cm). White with speckles and stripes of rose red. Also pale pink flowers with white margins and dark blotch. Occasional solid red selfs.
Note: Plants so far available in Britain have only shown the pale pink and red self variations.

Gyoten
[Dawn Sky]

(G.) (T.S. page 746)

Sport of Kaho

Rich pink. Some blooms have darker pink sectors. Blotch is yellowish-green, changing to deep crimson when in a darker sector. Occasional blooms will revert to white/pink Kaho type. Round wavy petals, (6cm-7cm). Dense growth habit which Galle describes as slow. Though slower growing than Kaho, most people would still consider it quite vigorous.

Hakurei
[White Excellence]

(G) (T.S. page 62)

Kozan X Osakazuki

White star-shaped flowers with narrow pointed petals, (3.5cm-4cm). Faint, pale pink blotch. Very slow bushy growth.

Hi-Gasa
[Parasol]

(G) (T.S. page 451)

Banko X Shinnyo-no-Tsuki

Rich purplish-pink flowers with rose blotch. Very large, wide, wavy petals, (10cm-12.5cm) which have a tendency to curve backwards. Vigorous upright growth habit.

Hiodoshi
[Scarlet-Threaded Suit of Armour]

(G) (T. S. page 132)

Good "sokojiro" form (pale centre with dark margin). Flowers are a strong red with the centre being white or slightly pink. Slightly bell-shaped with round-ended, spaced lobes, (5cm-6.5cm). Medium to vigorous, upright growth.
Note: Very prone to bark-splitting when subjected to prolonged frost.

Hinotsukasa
[Vermillion Official]

(G.) (T.S. page 98)

Ancient variety

Dark reddish-orange with darker red blotch. Lobes very evenly spaced and slightly pointed.(5cm-7.5cm).

Kaho
[Floral Treasure]

(G.) (T.S. page 546)

Seedling of Asahizuru.

White with occasional deep pink stripes, and some light to dark pink selfs. Also, light pink with white border. Wavy rounded petals, (6cm-7.5cm). Vigorous upright growth.

Kanuma-no-Hikari
[Light of Kanuma]

(G.) (T.S. page 187)

Gyoko x Hoshi.

White flowers are marked with many patterns of flecks, stripes and speckles in reddish-orange. Occasional reddish-orange selfs. Very variable. Petals slightly pointed, (6cm-7.5cm). Upright growth with larger than average leaves.

Karenko

(T.S. page 742)

Seedling of Juko.

White bordered light pink to strong rose-red with many variations. Spaced, pointed petals, (4cm-5cm). Upright growth of medium vigour.

Kazan
[Deer Mountain]

(G.) (T.S. page 77)

Sport of Taihai.

Small neat flowers of pale pinkish-red (3.5cm-5cm). Prominent blotch and black-tipped stamens. Leaves are very small, dark green and somewhat heart-shaped. Branches are more flexible than on most Satsuki varieties.

Kinsai
[Golden Tassel]

(G.) (T.S. page 83)

Ancient variety

The classic "Saizaki" variety, (described by Ito in the 1690s under the name Zai. Flowers are deep reddish-orange with petals being long narrow and contorted (4cm-6cm). Stamens are very long and prominent. Plants also bear some flowers with full rounded petals. This variety has a low spreading growth habit.

Kobai
[Red Plum]

(G) (T.S. page 475)

Sanko-no-Tsuki X Yata-no-Kagami

Strong cerise pink. Flowers on mature plants develop distinctive white blotches. Rounded, overlapping petals, (3.5cm-5cm).

Kogetsu
[Monthly Tribute]

(G) (T.S. page 215)

Matsunami X Tamaorihime

White with bold stripes of strong red, to white with a red border. Occasionally pink with deep crimson blotch and narrow white border. One of the most spectacular Satsuki. "Many beautiful variations!" (Galle). Wide overlapping lobes, (5cm-6.5cm).

Komei
[Brilliant Light]

(G) (T.S. page 579)

Kozan X Tamaorihime

Many variations of pink flecks and stripes on a white ground. Also deep pink selfs and some light pink with darker blotch. Very neat flowers with spaced petals, (3.5cm-5cm).

Korin
[Name of a famed Japanese artist]

(G) (T.S. page 429)

Kozan X Osakazuki.

Deep rose-pink. Star shaped with pointed petals (3.5cm-5cm). The medium vigour combined with very compact growth and small flower size make this variety very desirable for bonsai.

Kozan
[Brilliant Mountain]

(G) (T.S. page 803)

Ancient variety.

Very pale pink to off-white. Very neat flower with spaced, rounded petals, (4cm). Variable and very prone to sporting different colours, flower forms, petal numbers, etc. Very slow bushy growth.

Kozan-no-Hikari
[Light of Kozan]

(G) (T.S. page 804)

Sport of Kozan

Flowers light peach-pink fading to white. Star-shaped with long pointed lobes, (3.5cm-5cm). (Flower form and size seem quite variable.)

Kusudama
[Camphor-tree Gem]

(G.) (T.S. page 748)

Sport of Shinnyo-no-Tsuki

Pale pink overlaid with many variations of deep pink flecks, speckles and sectors. Occasional flowers are deep pink solids and blooms with a pale centre and pink border also occur. Round, wavy petals, (6.5cm-7.5cm). Vigorous growth habit.

Nachi-no-Tsuki
[Moon of Nachi]

(G.) (T.S. page656)

Shiko-no-Tsuki X Chiyo-no-Tsuki

White, striped and flecked with many variations of strong purplish-red. Purplish-red selfs also occur. Neat bell-shaped flowers with narrowly-spaced lobes,(4cm-6cm)

Nyohozan
[Mount Nyoho]

(G) (T.S. page 936)

Sport of Kozan

Pale pink with vivid red blotch in throat. Spaced lobes, (3cm-5cm). Very slow growth.

Nikko
[Sunlight]

(G) (T.S. page 885)

Sport of Kozan

Base colour varies from strong pink to very pale pink. Varied amounts of white or pale pink striping. Occasional selfs of deep reddish-pink. Spaced lobes, (3cm-5cm). Slow growing.

Osakazuki
[Large Sake Cup]

(G) (T.S. page 72)

Ancient variety.

Classic bonsai variety. Deep rose pink flowers with darker blotch, (5cm-6cm).

Polo

This is an American bred Satsuki with brilliant blood red flowers, some with white centres, (5cm). Among the most stunning of red Satsuki.

Shinnyo-no-Tsuki
[Eternal Moon]

(G) (T.S. page 483)

Sakuragata X Zetsurin

Reliable *sokojiro* type flower with vivid purplish-pink margins and white centres. Occasional pink selfs. Wide overlapping petals, (7cm-9cm).

Shira-Fuji
[White Mount Fuji]

(G) (T.S. page 614)

Sport of Aikoku.

White with some speckles and stripes of purplish pink. Occasional selfs in purplish-pink or purple. Flower form somewhat irregular, (3.5cm-5cm).
NOTE: This variety is most noted for its variegated foliage; green, bordered creamy white.

Shiraito-no-Taki
[White-Thread Waterfall]

(G) (T.S. page 39)

Origin unknown.

Extreme "Saizaki" form. White with an occasional purplish stripe. Flowers are very irregular with some or all petals missing on most blooms and the white stamens are very distinct.

Shiryu-no-Homare
[Glory of the Purple Dragon]

(T.S. page 441)

Purple flowers with narrow pointed spider petals, (5cm-7cm). Unusual slender twisted (Rinpu-type) foliage.

Shuho-no-Hikari
[Light of Excellent Peak]

(G) (T.S. page 933)

Sport of Kozan-no-Hikari.

Attractive strong pink, often with paler edges to petals. Strong red blotch. Star-shaped with narrow, spaced, pointed petals, (3.5cm-5cm). Slow bushy growth

Tatsunami
[High Wave]

(T.S. page 290)

Ancient variety.

The petals are deeply divided and give the distinct impression of being "squared off" at the tips compared with other Satsuki flowers. Most flowers have a white base colour while others are lighter or darker orangey-red. The white flowers have variable amounts of orange-red striping, (4cm-5cm).

Ungetsu-no-Hana
[Flower of the Cloudy Moon]

(G.) (T.S. page 71)

Origin Unknown.

Medium size trumpet-shaped blooms with spaced petals in a rich salmon pink, (5cm-6.5cm).
NOTE: This appears to be a different plant to that described by Galle.

Ungetsu-no-Hikari
[Light of the Cloudy Moon]

(G.) (T.S. page 929)

Origin Unknown.

Pink, fading to pale pink at edges of petals. Strong blotch with distinct red dots. Small flowers with spaced, pointed petals, (4cm-5cm). Slow bushy growth.

Wakaebisu
[Young Goddess]

(G.) (T.S. page 810)

Origin Unknown.

Warm pink with distinct dark pink dots in blotch. Hose-in-hose type with open, rounded form, (5cm-6cm).
Note: This beautiful plant is the only hose-in-hose type commonly used for bonsai in Japan.

Yata-no-Sai
[Sacred Tassel]

(G) (T.S. page 139)

Sport of Yata-no-Kagami

Blush pink to deep coral colour is the same as Yata-no-Kagami. Most flowers show varying amounts of narrowing and distortion of the petals. Extreme flowers have long narrow saizaki-type form while on others the bulk of the petal is missing, leaving a tiny "lily-of-the-valley" shaped stub. (5cm-6cm).

Yata-no-Kagami
[Sacred Mirror]

(G) (T.S. page 138)

Origin unknown. From Meiji era (1868-1912).

Blush pink centres shading to deep coral round edges. Some flowers deeper coloured with same pattern, others are coral selfs with dark blotch. Spaced petals, (5cm-6cm).

Further Reading

General texts on azaleas

Azaleas; by Fred C. Galle; Timber Press, 1987

This huge book is the standard monograph on azalea species and their hybrids. A chapter on Satsuki is included, with a long descriptive list of many varieties available in the U.S.A.

Books on Satsuki

Satsuki; written and published by Alexander Kennedy, 1995

A Brocade Pillow - Azaleas of Old Japan (translation of Kinshi Makura); by Ito Ihei; (translation by Kaname Kato; commentary by John L. Creech); Weatherhill 1984

Bonsai Techniques For Satsuki; by John Y. Naka, Richard K. Ota and Kenko Rokkaku; Ota Bonsai Nursery, 1979

Glossary

Akadama

Japanese red-clay, granular potting soil widely used for bonsai.

Apical dominance

The tendency of most plants to concentrate their growing energies at the tallest point. Satsuki are, by contrast, basally dominant; in other words they concentrate their energies on the outward spread of their lowest shoots.

Branch sports

This refers to genetic mutations occurring within an individual plant, so that certain branches exhibit different characteristics from the rest. If a Satsuki branch sport can be reliably propagated by vegetative means, it may be given a new variety name of its own.

Cut-paste

A Japanese compound for sealing tree wounds. It promotes rapid healing of large wounds and the new callous growth is able to spread under the paste.

Evergreen garden azaleas

The evergreen, spring-flowering azaleas

commonly grown in British gardens. Also called Japanese azaleas. In Japan these azaleas are called *Tsutsuji*.

Ito Ihei

A gardener and nurseryman of the early Edo era. His monograph on azaleas, the Kinshi Makura (1692), was almost certainly the world's first book devoted to a single group of plants.

Kanuma

A yellowish, acid sub-soil dug in the region of Kanuma city in Japan.

Kinshi Makura (A Brocade Pillow)

Book by Ito Ihei on the subject of azaleas. This was the first work to systematically divide azaleas into *Tsutsuji* and Satsuki.

Kiyonal

A Japanese wound-sealant.

Meika

Satsuki trained and exhibited for the appreciation of the flowers only. Normally grown in the Repeated "S" style.

Miracid

A widely-available soluble fertilizer and soil-acidifier; used for all ericaceous plants, and recommended for Satsuki.

Shohin

Very small, easily portable bonsai.

Sports

Genetically altered plants with characteristics which distinguish them from the parent variety or type.

Trace elements

Nutrient elements required by plants in very small amounts. Micronutrients are generally supplied in chelated form, which means they are specially prepared to be easily taken up by the plant roots. In addition to the major nutrients (Nitrogen, Phosphorous and Potassium), azaleas need small quantities of Iron, Magnesium, Manganese and Boron.

Satsuki require trace elements in very small quantities indeed and it is very easy to create a fresh set of problems through overdose.

Tsutsuji

Spring-flowering evergreen azaleas.

Note:

Meanings of the Japanese terms for the various flower patterns are discussed in Chapter 5.

Index

A
A Brocade Pillow 23
Air-Layering 127
Akadama 157
apex 114, 149
aphids 161
Arare-shibori 70
azalea gall 162

B
back-budding 116, 117
bark 48, 141
bark splitting 163
basic branch structure 150
Belgian-Indian hybrids 30
Biogold 159
blotch 61, 62
bonsai 44
branch sports 128
branch structure 119, 148

C
calcined clay (e.g. "Biosorb") 157
Colour-Ring Variations 63
Creation of a Satsuki Bonsai 134
Cut-Paste 120, 164
cuttings 124, 125, 126, 129

D
Daisho-shibori 67
Date-shibori 68
development of young plants 138

E
Exhibiting Satsuki 11

F
fertilizer 102, 145, 158
flower buds 103, 108, 139
flower structure 54
flower types 55
flowering performance 119
flowering period 160
Fukiage-shibori 69
Fukkake-shibori 70
Fukurin 64
fungal diseases 98, 162
fungicide 162

G
Gamma BHC powder 161

H
Hakeme-shibori 69
Hanzome 66
hard tap water 158
hardiness 29, 164
Harusame 71
Hedge Satsuki (see Magaki Satsuki)

I
indentifying Satsuki branches 131
initial trunk shaping 141
insecticide 161
insulating fleece 98, 164
Ito Ihei 23, 77

J
Janome-shibori 64
Japanese gardens 16, 22, 34

K
Kanji 24, 91
Kanuma city 76
Kanuma Satsuki Centre 79
Kanuma Satsuki Festival 87, 93
Kanuma soil 76, 125, 148
Kanuma-tsuchi (see Kanuma soil) 156
Kiyonal 164
Ko-shibori 66
Kokufu 50

L
leaves 26, 29, 46, 139, 141, 158
lime 156, 158

M

Magaki Satsuki 35
Maintaining colour patterns 72
Masahiko Kimura 50
Meika 46, 87, 93, 147
Mie Satsuki 35
Mijin-shibori 71
Miracid 158, 159
mutations 130

N

National Satsuki Festival 87
nematodes 161
new varieties 89

O

O-shibori 66

P

peat 125, 156
pests 161
pH 156
phosphoric acid 158
poor ventilation 162
pot-bound bonsai 119
propagating true-to-type 128
propagation 123, 124, 168
pruning 97, 104, 145, 152
pumice 125, 157

R

R. eriocarpum (see R. tamurae)
R. lateritum (see R. indicum)
rainwater 158
raw material 135
Red Spider Mite 161
removal of flower buds 140
repotting 104
response to pruning 36, 49, 145
Rhododendron indicum 26
Rhododendron tamurae 26, 59
river satsuki (see R. indicum) 26
root rot 156, 162
root system 145
round-leaved satsuki (see R. tamurae)

S

saizaki 55, 130
sap withdrawal 118, 146
Satsuki care cycle 98
Satsuki exhibition classes 88
Satsuki magazines 13
Satsuki nurseries in Japan 81
seed 107, 124
selfs 61, 129
Sequestrene 159
severe pruning of very large plants 118
Shibori 65, 72, 129
Shiro-shibori 68
Shohin 91, 149
show Satsuki in the garden 39
soil 27, 145, 156
Sokojiro 63, 129
sphagnum moss 127, 148, 157
spring re-potting 100
striped flower 129
styling 46, 50, 143, 146
surface roots 47, 142

T

Tamafu 65
Tate-shibori 67
The Great Azalea Vogue 22
the move to a training pot 146
tie-dye 65
Tokonoma display 19
trace elements 158, 159
training pot 134, 146, 147, 148
trimming new shoots 112
trunks 14, 47, 135, 140, 147
Tsumabeni 63
Tsutsuji 18, 24, 41

V

variegated 185
variety names 168
Vine Weevil 161

W

water 103, 145, 158
winter protection 163
wiring 100, 104, 120, 141, 147